# The
# Language Laboratory
# and
# Language Learning

## Julian Dakin

## Longman

LONGMAN GROUP LTD
London
*Associated companies, branches and
representatives throughout the world*

First published 1973
Second impression 1975

ISBN 0 582 55228 1

Printed in Great Britain by
Lowe & Brydone (Printers) Ltd, Thetford, Norfolk

ACKNOWLEDGEMENTS

We are grateful to the following for
permission to reproduce extracts from
their work.
Adaptation of excerpt from "East Coker"
in Four Quartets by T. S. Eliot is reprinted by permission of Harcourt Brace
Jovanovich Inc.; copyright 1943 by T. S.
Eliot; copyright 1971 by Esme Valerie
Eliot. The same adaptation of an excerpt
from "East Coker" in Four Quartets from
*Collected Poems 1909–1962* is reprinted
by permission of Faber and Faber Ltd.

# Contents

# Author's Note

Without Libby Joyce and Dorothy Forrester this book would never have taken shape. Miss Joyce, a Lecturer at the University College of the West Indies, first made me wonder what structural drills actually practise, and whether they practise structures at all. Miss Forrester, a Lecturer at Doncaster College of Education, and formerly a teacher of French at Boroughmuir School, Edinburgh, first showed me that there were meaningful alternatives to structural drills in the language laboratory.

I am also indebted to a number of former students at the Department of Applied Linguistics, Edinburgh, who have inspired me by producing types of drills I had never seen before. In this paper, I have reproduced some of these drills as examples, indicating in the footnotes the identity of their original designer.

Nirupam Chatterjee has checked my Bengali examples, and Sachin Ganguly has helped to improve my understanding of the exercise of verification and falsification.

The style and format of many of my own illustrative materials owe a great deal to the example of Anthony Howatt, my colleague at Edinburgh, whose advice and encouragement have greatly improved every successive version of this paper. It was he, too, who first introduced me to Novish, and who helped me to describe it.

The style of the text has considerably benefited from suggestions and criticism made by my father and by Peter O'Connell, the director of the School of English Studies in Folkestone.

J. D.

Calcutta, June 1969 and Edinburgh, September 1971.

# Preface

Julian Dakin did not live to see his book through the final stages of publication. He had, however, passed the manuscript to a number of his friends and colleagues for their comments and suggestions for improvement. Some of these comments had been returned to him and he had added his own notes to them. Provided his intentions were clear and small changes could be made without altering the main body of the text, I have tried to incorporate them. He would I am sure have wished to acknowledge the assistance of his colleague at Edinburgh, Dr Gillian Brown, his father Mr S. Dakin and Miss Dorothy Forrester, mentioned in his own Acknowledgements, for their valuable and perceptive comments on the final manuscript. There is no doubt that he wished the book to be published and considered it ready. Though he might perhaps have altered the emphasis and balance of certain passages, he would I think have made no changes of substance or content. But any errors arising during the final stages of publication and printing are of course mine.

A. H.

Edinburgh, 1972.

# The role of the language laboratory

*Oh, let us never, never doubt*
*What nobody is sure about!*
    HILAIRE BELLOC

## 1 The aims of this book

This book is concerned with relating two themes: the uses of the language laboratory and the nature of language learning. In recent years language laboratories have spread widely and rapidly. They can now be found in schools as well as in adult education centres. At the same time a large number of books and courses has come on to the market advocating or embodying differing methods of instruction in the language laboratory. Protagonists of one particular method of approach or another sometimes suggest that the general principles of language teaching are clear enough and that their own materials, based on these principles, provide a more effective means to language learning. It is certainly true that the materials commercially available can be used to good effect. But it has yet to be shown that any single course or method of approach is reliably more effective than others. Equally good, and at times equally disappointing, results can be attributed to courses based on different general principles. And although the language laboratory has attained a certain level of popularity among both teachers and students, it is still not clear whether laboratory instruction is more effective than work in the classroom.

Valid principles of language learning, far from being clear and easy to apply, are still for the most part tantalisingly obscure. Far from being well-established, the role and value of the language laboratory has still to be determined. This book cannot resolve these issues for the reader. Its aim rather is to explore them in order to define the limits of our uncertainties. The teacher who does not possess a laboratory may learn something of what he could expect from one. The teacher who already possesses one is shown how he could use it most fully. And, for the teacher who wants to design his own materials, a large number of sample materials are illustrated. The scope of each type of drill or exercise is indicated so that he can create further materials to suit the particular problems of his own pupils.

This book is not a manual of instructions for operating a language laboratory. Various manuals about the selection, maintenance, and technical use of equipment are already in existence. Nor does the book offer the reader a programme of language laboratory work, though two strategies of laboratory use are developed in the final chapter. The aim is rather to present an illustrated encyclopaedia of laboratory teaching techniques. My assumption is that the reader already knows, or can find out elsewhere, *what* he wants to teach his pupils. His interest in the laboratory lies rather in *how* it can further his aims. He is also naturally concerned with *how far* it can further them. To help him make up his own mind about this, the possible limitations of each kind of laboratory technique are exposed at length at the end of each chapter or section.

Finally, the book tries to give the reader the experience of learning in the ways in which it is suggested he might teach. He is given sample lessons in two unfamiliar languages, and the English examples are presented in such a way that he can work through them himself. The language laboratory, as its name suggests, is a place for experiment. And we can try experiments on ourselves as well as on our pupils. By experimenting with our pupils we can find out whether something works as well as we intended it to do. By observing and reflecting on our own problems and failures as learners, we can seek to establish principles which will help us to improve our teaching. Our success in teaching is dependent on our understanding of learning.

This book, then, will switch from looking at teaching materials to looking at learners, and will invite the reader to become a learner himself. For this purpose, it matters little whether he has used a laboratory before or ever intends to use one. Whatever we can learn about learning is of value however we intend to teach. And any teaching materials in this book that capture the reader's interest can be adapted as readily to classroom use as to the laboratory. The availability of a laboratory merely raises the question of where they can be tried out most effectively. For the laboratory offers certain facilities that cannot be reproduced in the classroom.

## 2  The nature of the language laboratory

These facilities are most fully exemplified in a laboratory in which every student has his own tape-recorder. The tape-recorder is equipped with earphones which enable the student to listen to the material recorded on his own tape without disturbing the rest of the class. Through a microphone he can also record his own voice. He can play back his recording to check for mistakes or to compare his own efforts with a model version already recorded on the tape. There is a connecting channel between the teacher and the student so that the former can listen to what the student is doing and discuss any problems with him without interrupting the work of other pupils.

The effect of the machinery is to isolate each learner from his fellows in several different ways:

**1. Each learner can work all the time.** He no longer has to sit idly while other pupils answer questions or show the teacher what they can do. He can work uninterruptedly either at listening to material on his own tape or at trying to improve his speech.

**2. Each learner can work at his own pace.** He no longer needs to be either held back or out-stripped by the pace of learning of the rest of the class. He can stop the tape whenever he is in doubt, replay each section as many times as he wishes, and repeat each exercise till he is satisfied with his performance.

**3. Each learner can work on his own materials.** There is no longer any need for him to listen to the same materials or do all the same exercises as the rest of the class. He can be given work which matches his own needs and interests.

**4. Each learner is responsible for his own performance.** He is spared the embarrassment of having other pupils listening to all his mistakes. Instead he must learn to correct himself when he goes wrong, and to seek advice from the teacher when he is in doubt.

**5. Each learner receives individual attention from the teacher.**

It is easier to list these possibilities than to exploit them. They present a formidable task to a teacher who attempts to do so. He must have a sufficient amount of material to keep each of his pupils uninterruptedly engaged. But he cannot expect them all to do the same amount of work during the laboratory periods and should adjust any follow-up in the classroom accordingly. In addition to a common core of work which he may want all his pupils to do at some time, he must provide a whole library of ancillary materials for learners with special difficulties or interests. Since he cannot give too much of his time to any single student, he must design the materials so that each can learn on his own with a minimum of supervision. Difficulties, misunderstandings and mistakes which could be dealt with as they arose in the classroom must as far as possible be anticipated or forestalled in the design of laboratory materials. Every step must be planned and recorded in advance.

The laboratory thus frees the student at the cost of tying the teacher. It makes instruction more individual, but at the same time more impersonal. To use it effectively, it must be determined what a student can learn better on his own with only occasional supervision from the teacher, and what requires interaction between the student and the teacher, or between one student and another, and is therefore more suitable for the classroom. We must decide, in effect, what can be planned in advance and performed in isolation, and what should be improvised in face-to-face contact.

# 3   What can be done in the language laboratory?

Could we, for instance, do all our teaching in the laboratory? Just what would this involve? When we are teaching something new, whether it is a grammatical point or a poem, the "whole" teaching process can be divided into four stages:

1. Presentation

2. Practice

3. Development

4. Testing

We can examine each stage in turn to decide how far responsibility for it could be effectively delegated to the language laboratory.

## 4 Presentation

A teacher presenting a new grammatical point, for example, can adopt one of two techniques: *demonstration* or *involvement*.[1] In either case he wants to give the pupils examples of the new structure or rule. He can *demonstrate* its meaning by presenting the examples in isolation or, at the most, in contrast with something already known but easily confused. Both the isolation and the contrast are intended to call the pupils' attention to the novelty of the point. The teacher is saying in effect: "Here is something new". He hopes to make its meaning clear by mime, pictures, or translation, or by providing a minimal context.

If he prefers the technique of *involvement,* he will not tell the pupils that he is going to use a new structure, but will slip examples of it into something else he is saying in such a way that it will be understood and accepted quite naturally. The past tense, for example, can be unobtrusively but appropriately introduced in telling stories to the class. The teacher can sometimes even get the pupils to "invent" the structure themselves. A class of children involved in drawing or painting, for example, will sooner or later demand more paper or more paint. At this point, when the demand is freshly felt but as yet unexpressable in the new language, the teacher can slip onto the tips of the pupils' tongues such structures as "I want X", or "Can I have some more Y?".

Demonstration and involvement both require interaction between teacher and pupils.

## 5 Practice

Having presented examples of the new structure or rule, the teacher must now go on to practise it. This means getting the pupils to produce their own examples in response to some question or cue. The nature of the different kinds of cues that can be used will be discussed in the chapters on drills. What concerns us immediately is that the techniques of practice, as they are practised in the classroom, once again require interaction between teacher and pupils. The teacher listens to what the pupils say, approving or emending, and the pupils have to note both the teacher's cues for the next response and his reactions to the last one. Where there is a breakdown in their responses, the teacher can present the point again or give further examples. He can also provide explanations in the new language or, if need be, in the mother tongue. At this stage, and in the next one, a pupil's actual responses are often unexpected or confused. He may have difficulty in formulating the new structure or he may betray that he has misunderstood its meaning.

## 6 Development

This is the stage when the teacher has to relax control over the pupils' performance. The pupils are set tasks such as telling a story themselves, describing pictures, retailing their daily lives and past or future activities, expressing their own needs and preferences. The successful completion of such tasks calls for the use not only of the structure that has just been practised but of all that has been learnt before. The teacher cannot and should not interrupt the pupils' performance by correcting every single mistake. He can indicate that he does not understand, he can prompt where the pupil falters and he can override him when he pauses for breath, but many slips made in the flow of utterance can only be dealt with later, if at all. The stage of development thus involves its own kind of interaction between the pupil and his audience — the interaction of real conversation — but for the first time the pupil can select the cues to which he will respond. As far as organising and developing his own utterances is concerned, he is largely on his own.

## 7 Testing

When the teacher comes to formally testing what the pupils have learnt, he must relax control altogether and leave the pupils entirely on their own. This is essential if the test is to be a fair one of what has been learnt, what still needs to be learnt, and what has to be taught again.

## 8 Stages of teaching and stages of learning

Let us take a closer look at what the pupil is doing while the teacher is busy presenting, practising, developing and testing. In the last two stages, I have suggested that the pupil is increasingly on his own. But surely he is always on his own? We may teach a class, but each pupil has to learn for himself. If we look at the whole teaching process from the pupil's point of view, we can see that it also falls into four stages, each corresponding to the changing intentions of the teacher.

When the teacher presents the new point, the pupil has to *understand* it. When the teacher practises the point, the pupil has to *learn* it. And when the teacher seeks to exploit the newly acquired knowledge, the pupil has to *control* it.[2] As we have seen, any developmental task may call upon all that he has already learnt. In addition, it requires him to express himself not just correctly, but well.

For the pupil, if not for the teacher, testing is a continuous process, co-extensive and co-terminous with everything he does. Each effort to understand tests his intelligence and his knowledge of the language. Each effort to speak tests his memory of the rules and his ability to apply them in response to new cues or new situations. As long as he has the teacher's attention, he can immediately find out whether he is right or wrong. Formal tests, however, have little extra value for the pupil, though they may stimulate him to learn. For a formal test cannot usually be allowed to give the pupil immediate and detailed information about how well he is doing.

To summarise and contrast what has been said about the stages of learning and the stages of teaching, every step in the teaching process requires continual interaction between teacher and pupil, while every step in the learning process requires continual effort on the part of the pupil. We must now ask whether all the teaching stages can be automatized — that is, taken over by a mechanical device such as the language laboratory. There is no need to pose the same question about the learning stages. If learning were always automatic, we would never have any failures.

## 9  The learner's problems

Some degree of failure is a universal consequence of trying to teach. Our interest in the language laboratory stems precisely from the hope that, by allowing each pupil to work at his own pace on his own materials, we may thereby reduce the margin of frustration and failure. But we will be no more successful at doing so in the laboratory unless we can first identify, and then attempt to forestall, the causes of the learner's failures.

We have seen that teaching is a spirally evolving process of presentation, practice, development and testing, while learning reflects it with its own progression of understanding, learning and control. The reflection is often distorted because each step confronts the pupil with a different kind of problem. At the stage of *presentation/understanding,* there is *the problem of meaning.* How can the teacher convey, how can the pupil grasp, the meaning of the new item? On a correct understanding of its meaning depends the successful application of the item to appropriate situations. At the stage of *practice/learning,* there is the problem of *remembering.* How can teacher and learner ensure that the new item will not be forgotten when the need for it arises in real situations? At the stage of *development/control,* there is the problem of *communication.* How can the teacher teach, the learner learn, the skill of effective communication in continually novel situations? Communication is essentially personal, the expression of personal needs, feelings, experiences and knowledge, in situations that are never quite the same. And though we may often repeat ourselves, much of our conversation about even the most mundane matters is to some degree novel. We hear or produce utterances that we have never heard or produced before in quite the same form, and which, in consequence, cannot be practised by the teacher or previously learnt by the learner. "My guinea pig died with its legs crossed", said one eight year old girl in a tape-recorded interview.[3] No teacher is going to present such an utterance as serious material for drilling in the classroom or laboratory. The example simply reveals that we can never anticipate everything that our pupils want to say.

This discussion of teaching and learning stages may seem to have led us away from the question from which we started: What can be done in the language laboratory? But I hope it is now clear that it is not the teacher's problems we must solve in the laboratory but the learner's.

## 10   The role of the language laboratory

Let us accordingly rephrase the question as: *Can the language laboratory solve the problems of meaning, remembering and communication?*

Some experts think it can handle all three kinds of problem, some only two, or perhaps one. One teacher of Spanish,[4] for example, gave his whole course in the laboratory, using specially programmed materials. Various courses for the teaching of English, French, Spanish, German and Bengali, present new material in the laboratory and practise it there but leave its development to the teacher in the classroom.[5] Finally, several recent British courses for Spanish, German and English use the laboratory principally for practice, rather than for presentation or development.[6]

The common feature of these various approaches is the concentration on practice in the laboratory. The learner is made to repeat or learn by heart selected words, phrases, sentences or conversations. He is also given a variety of structural drills or role-playing exercises which encourage him to manipulate what he is learning. The full range of such techniques of practice is listed in the next section of this chapter. Subsequent chapters investigate how far these techniques of practice are effective in the laboratory. Let us here pause to consider the adequacy of the laboratory in tackling the problems of understanding and communication.

When we present new material in the classroom, for instance, we have the opportunity of watching our pupils' faces, of questioning them, of expanding and renewing our attempts to convey meaning. In the laboratory we can use pictures, translation and explanation for this purpose, but once we have incorporated these into a particular taped lesson, we have no immediate means of amplifying them should unforeseen misunderstandings occur. But pictures can all too easily be misread,[7] explanations misinterpreted, and translations misapplied.[8]

The laboratory is also more restricted than the classroom as a means of development. Though it is possible to communicate something new to the student via the tape-recorder, it is quite impossible for the tape-recorder to react to anything the student says. Only one half of the process of communication can be reproduced. For true dialogue, we need at least two human beings. We do not need a tape-recorder.

## 1 1  Forms of practice

In this book, accordingly, the laboratory will be considered primarily as a
practising device. Material already introduced in class can be revised and
learned more thoroughly. The student's understanding of spoken language
can also be developed in the laboratory and his control over new material
rehearsed in simulated dialogues in which at least one side of the conversation has been fixed in advance. But the principal task of the laboratory
must be to help the student learn what has been initially introduced in the
classroom. For this purpose there are at least six different forms of
practice:

1. Listening

2. Meaningless drills

3. Meaningful drills

4. Comprehension exercises

5. Production exercises

6. Problems

"Listening" is to be distinguished from "comprehension exercises" in
that it elicits no overt reaction from the learner. He simply listens to
something in the laboratory, as he would listen to a record or to the radio.
Listening can be an end in itself, a means of learning something new, and
an aid to remembering something half-learnt. "Production exercises" differ
from drills in that the former require the learner to produce sentences of
differing grammatical type, while the latter prompt only sentences of identical or related structure. A classroom example of an exercise is prose
translation; a substitution table is the most familiar form of drill. Substitution tables are also a good illustration of "meaningless drills". Many
authors call such drills structural drills, pattern drills, or pattern practice. I
am not certain that such drills do in fact practise structures or patterns,
and I want to leave this question open for further discussion. What is
certainly clear, however, is that they are meaningless. A learner possessing
not the slightest knowledge of the language could produce a whole series
of correct sentences – if we ignore his pronunciation – from the following
"simple" substitution table:

| I    He | have   has | already     | seen   | it            |
|---------|------------|-------------|--------|---------------|
| You     |            | just        | heard  | them          |
| We She  |            | not  yet    | read   | books         |
| They    |            |             | eaten  | apples        |

His task, which permits no error, is merely to construct a sentence by
choosing one item from each column. Even if we make the substitution
table "complex" by introducing items like *he* and *she* into the first

agreement between the noun & the verb

column, and *has* into the second, the learner could get all the sentences
right, without understanding the meaning of any of them, provided only
that he knows one grammatical rule concerning "agreement" between pronoun and verb. Only when we add vocabulary items like *the book, the
record, the film, the apple,* to the last column have we set the learner a
task which for its successful completion requires a knowledge of at least
one kind of meaning relationship in the language. If he chooses to say, for
example:

I have just eaten the record,

or

He has already read the apple,

we cannot correct such utterances without explaining something of the
meaning of the words *eat, read, record* and *apple.*

All the forms of practice so far referred to give opportunities for either
understanding or producing sentences. Some practise both. Into the latter
category must go the final form of practice in the list: "problems".
Problem solving is as much a technique of presentation as of practice. An
example of a language learning problem that learners of English have to
face at an early stage is the use of the two forms of the indefinite article, *a*
and *an.* Here the teacher can readily formulate a rule. But he may not be
able to communicate it to his pupils, either because he does not know the
words for consonant and vowel in their mother tongue or because his
pupils, if very young, may not know them either. By a judicious use of
example, encouragement and correction, the teacher can nonetheless help
his pupils to induce the rule productively in much the same way that
young English children do. The art of problem setting lies in selecting and
presenting examples in such a way that the learners are first made aware
that there is a problem and are then guided through any necessary stages
towards its solution.

In this chapter, I have suggested that every use of the laboratory must
prove itself by its results. It is unlikely that it can satisfactorily replace the
teacher in the classroom altogether. The effectiveness of our teaching
might be impaired rather than improved if we relied exclusively on the
laboratory for presenting or developing new material. In these areas
personal interaction and improvisation are indispensable. The value of the
laboratory must rather be ascertained as a means of giving concentrated
individual practice. Six forms of practice have now been outlined. In
subsequent chapters we shall study each in detail. But the next chapter
turns aside to look at learners and at what it is that we are trying to teach
them to do. For there is little point in discussing *how* we can practise
something unless we are clear about *what* we want to practise and *why* we
think it is worthwhile practising it in that particular way.

NOTES

1.  For techniques of presenting new vocabulary items, see S. P. Corder: "The Teaching of Meaning", in *Applied Linguistics and the Teaching of English*, ed. Fraser and O'Donnell, Longman, 1969. For techniques of presenting poems, see A. Rodger's two papers in the same volume and P. Edwards: *Ballad Book for Africa*, Faber and Faber 1968 "Meaning and Context: An Exercise in Practical Stylistics", *English Language Teaching* XXII/3, May 1968.
2.  These terms are taken from David Bradley: *An Investigation of Reading*, dissertation for the Diploma in Applied Linguistics, Edinburgh, 1966.
3.  R. J. Handscombe: "Linguistics and Children's Interests", in *Applied Linguistics and the Teaching of English*, op. cit.
4.  F. Rand Morton: *The Language Laboratory as a Teaching Machine*, publications of the Language Laboratory, Ann Arbor, Michigan, 1961.
5.  For instance: *Basic Conversational French*, Holt, Rinehart and Winston, 1963; *Entender y Hablar*, Harcourt, Brace and World, 1961, and French and German Courses by the same publisher; *Direct Contact* IVAC; *Introduction to Bengali*, East-West Center Press, Honolulu.
6.  The *Ealing Course in Spanish*, Longman 1967; the *Ealing Course in German*, Longman 1969; *The Turners*, Longman for The British Council, 1969; *A Modern Course in Business English*, Oxford University Press, 1967.
7.  For a description of what can go wrong with pictures, and the principles of designing and using them effectively, see A. Wright: "The role of the artist in the Production of Visual Materials for Language Teaching", *International Journal of Educational Science*, Vol. 1, pp. 139–150, 1967.
8.  For a discussion of the problems of translation, see S. P. Corder, "The Teaching of Meaning", op. cit.

# 2 The nature of language learning

*Se miente más de la cuenta*
*Por falta de fantasía:*
*También la verdad se inventa.*[1]
— ANTONIO MACHADO

*Die Sprache lässt sich nicht eigentlich lehren,*
*sondern nur im Gemüthe wecken.*[2]
WILHELM VON HUMBOLDT

## 1  The conditions for language learning

In the last chapter I listed six forms of practice and proposed to illustrate
and evaluate the scope of each in the language laboratory. It might seem
logical to illustrate them first and evaluate them afterwards. But an examination of the nature of drills, exercises and problems will be more
informed and, I feel, more fruitful, if we can establish some general principles of teaching at the outset. Each form of practice may prove to have
its own part to play in the process of language learning. But before looking
at the parts, we might do well to look at the whole. This chapter, then, is
concerned with the nature of language learning. It presents two contrasting
theories of language learning that have been advanced by psychologists. It
relates these theories to the behaviour of some learners. And finally it gives
the reader the opportunity of studying his own performance in learning a
language.

Any enquiry into teaching is bound to be indirect. Teaching itself is an
indirect process. As von Humboldt says:

> We cannot teach a language; we can only create the conditions under
> which it will be learned.

But what are the conditions that promote learning? For guidance we can
turn to the psychologists who have studied learning. Broadly speaking they
offer us a choice between two sets of conditions, each of which is held to
be sufficient and necessary for learning to take place. The one set is
proposed by traditional behaviourists, the other by those psychologists
who can conveniently be called cognitive.[3]

## 2  The behaviourist's conditions

The behaviourist views of learning that concern us here can be summarised
in two laws and one principle:

1. The law of exercise

2. The law of effect

3. The principle of shaping

The first law states that for learning to take place an "organism" must be *responding* actively and repeatedly. The more often it responds, the better it will remember. The stimulus to which it responds is immaterial. It could be an electric shock, a bell, or a flashing light. The second law states that if the response is rewarded — by release from pain, or by food — learning will be more effective. In other words, what happens after each response, its consequence, is not immaterial. If the consequences are painful, learning might be inhibited. The law of effect leads to the doctrine of forestalling failures or mistakes and to the principle of "shaping". The organism's responses are "shaped", in Skinner's terminology, in a series of steps, each of which is small enough to be successfully reached from the one before, each of which can therefore be rewarded, and each of which cumulatively leads to the desired end-behaviour.

## 3  The behaviourist in the classroom

As far as classroom practice is concerned, the behavioural laws commonly assume the form of maxims:

1. Get the pupils to utter the same structural pattern repeatedly;

2. Get them to do so correctly, forestalling all mistakes;

3. Do this by grading the structural patterns, that is by arranging them in order and introducing only one at a time.

The optimal order in which the patterns should be arranged is arrived at after a consideration of such factors as ease of learning, intelligibility, frequency of use in the language in question, demonstrability, mother tongue differences etc.[4]

The twin instruments of the behavioural approach to language learning are thus repetition and drilling. Drilling, as we shall see, is in effect only a sophisticated form of repetition. The learner is made to repeat not a single sentence but a structural pattern, varying its constituents systematically. The structural drill "shapes" each successive response of the learner just as the structurally graded syllabus shapes his progress from one structure to the next.

The language laboratory is at first sight an ideal asset for the behaviourist teacher. By enabling each student to work full time on his own, it promotes a maximum of active response and repetition. Each correct response of the learner can be rewarded or confirmed by his hearing the right answer on the tape. The only problem seems to be to shape his responses successfully, in other words, to ensure that he makes no mistakes.

## 4 **Cognitive conditions**

Cognitive principles of learning can also conveniently be summarised under three headings:

1. The need for experience

2. The twin processes of assimilation and accommodation

3. Developmental stages

Relevant experience is taken as a pre-requisite for learning. The mind is conceived not as a *tabula rasa* (a clean slate) but as an entity with a potential for adapting itself. Piaget considers the process of *adaptation* to be two-way. On the one hand, the organism *assimilates* new experience to itself. On the other, it *accommodates* itself to new kinds of experience. These terms can be illustrated in the case of human hearing. There are sounds too high or too low for us to assimilate, no matter how hard we listen. We can readily assimilate and respond to the sounds of our own language without conscious effort. We can also hear the sounds of an unknown language, but we cannot assimilate them further until we have "accommodated" our ears to distinguishing between them and to organising them into words. Listening to a new language, as opposed to just hearing that someone is making peculiar sounds, involves the hearer in adapting his existing mental machinery and in learning new rules and concepts. Accommodation renders accessible what was previously unperceivable or unconceivable.

Piaget suggests that, in the case of the intellectual development of the child, the process of accommodation is determined not by what we may choose to teach, but by what he is capable of learning at a particular point. The child has, so to speak, his own inner syllabus which, given experience and encouragement, will lead him through successive developmental stages.

## 5 **The cognitive classroom**

The three cognitive principles have been most readily adopted in the primary school. As far as classroom practice is concerned, they may also assume the form of maxims:

*expose them*
1. **Give your children experience of the language they are learning.** Teach them rhymes, tell them stories, talk to them.

2. **Give them activities to do:** painting, modelling, playing games, composing playlets or stories. These will practise in new situations what has already been learnt (assimilation), and will create further situations for which their existing language resources are inadequate and must, accordingly, be modified or extended (accommodation).[5]

3. **Don't stick rigidly to a predetermined language syllabus.** Let the course the activities take, the occurrence of stimulating events in the environ-

ment, the varying needs of the children and the mistakes they make, influence the vocabulary and structures that are introduced or practised in each lesson.

The language laboratory would be used as an extension of the cognitive teacher's classroom. The pupils are accustomed to working on their own, or in small groups, with only occasional supervision from the teacher. In the laboratory, they merely continue to listen to stories, solve problems, perform comprehension and production exercises related to their needs and interests. Such kinds of exercise are not, of course, restricted to primary school pupils. Many similar exercises in Chapters 6 and 7 are intended for highly advanced learners.[6]

## 6   To drill or not to drill

Drills were not mentioned in this brief account of the cognitive approach. It is not impossible to fit them in. But they would be treated as a form of game — and one that requires some ingenuity to bring to life. Listening practice, exercises and problems are central to this approach. Drills are not. Here we have come to the first of a series of contrasts between behaviourist and cognitive methods of teaching.

A detailed investigation of the possibilities and limitations of drills is undertaken in Chapters 4 and 5. For the present we are concerned with general principles of teaching. And behind the differing attitudes to drills there does lie a question of principle. This concerns mistakes.

## 7   Are mistakes a bad thing?

The function of a drill, for the behaviourist teacher, is to permit the learner to repeat a structural pattern actively without making mistakes. Mistakes are regarded as undesirable. If they are not immediately corrected, they may be repeated with the result that the pupil learns an incorrect form. If he is corrected too often, the pupil may get discouraged. The best policy, therefore, is to forestall mistakes. To the cognitive teacher, mistakes have a vital part to play in the learning process. They tell the learner that he has got something new to learn. When all his attempts at self-correction in the light of his existing knowledge fail, he is forced to realise that he is facing a problem of accommodation. Let us look at an actual example.

## 8   Shanace and the passive

In an experiment[7], a nine year old Pakistani girl called Shanace was asked to listen to a story about a naughty dog. The story included several passive sentences such as:

1. The dog was chased by the farmer.
2. The sheep were chased by the dog.

3. The dog was chased by the cows.

4. The door was shut by Tom.

Shanace and her classmates were then asked to retell the story by answering a series of questions about "who chased whom?" etc. Shanace's versions of the first three sentences went as follows:

1. The dog chased the farmer.

2. The sheep chased the dog.

3. The dog chased the cows.

So far she had treated all the passive sentences as if they were active. This corresponded with her previous grammatical "knowledge" that the first noun in a sentence is both the subject and the agent. It led her to produce a version of the story which is just as plausible as the original. But the same strategy cannot safely be followed with the fourth sentence. It would produce a nonsensical sentence:

**4. The door shut Tom.**

Shanace hesitated, looking very unhappy. Finally she muttered something about "Tom doing it". Then of her own accord, she immediately went back to the beginning again and produced correct active versions of the original sentences. She had just discovered a new rule, the passive transformation.

## 9  The role of mistakes

This case-study of Shanace gives us a successfully solved example of a language teaching "problem". Problems, as we have noted, are one of the cognitive teacher's alternatives to drills. And an essential feature of a problem is that the learner should have the chance of making, and learning from, a mistake. We can now formulate the question of principle that is at stake. For the most effective teaching, according to the behavioural approach:

1. We must design our lessons and language laboratory tapes so as to prevent the learner making mistakes.

According to the cognitive approach:

2. We must design our lessons and language laboratory tapes so as to invite the learner to make the minimum number of mistakes consonant with, and conducive to, learning new rules.

Which attitude we adopt towards mistakes will not merely influence our view of the functions of drills and problems. It should inform the design of our whole language teaching syllabus.

## 10  External and internal syllabuses

The function of the graded syllabus in the behaviourist approach is to prevent mistakes. Only one structure is introduced at a time, and the successive structures are so ordered that the learner can proceed from one to the next with minimum difficulty. In the cognitive approach, the syllabus is conceived of as lying within the learner. The experiences the teacher provides, and the problems he sets, are attempts to make the potential actual.

The idea of an in-built syllabus may seem strange at first. We are accustomed to think that it is the teacher who determines the syllabus and not the learner. But there are two kinds of evidence which suggest that though the teacher may control the experiences the learner is exposed to, it is the learner who selects what is learnt from them.

There are, for example, certain difficulties of pronunciation and grammar that we cannot avoid introducing early in our teaching of a second language. No matter how thoroughly we drill these points, the learners may persist in making mistakes. But if we give up drilling and correction in despair, the mistakes often disappear after a period of time that varies with each learner. The case-study of Jeeto in Section 15 of this chapter illustrates a learner still confused about the correct formation of the present continuous tense in English even after months of repeated drilling. Her confusion eventually resolved itself without any further drilling. The learner often behaves as if he was not ready to master a particular form until certain other things, which we have chosen to present later, have been learnt.

The second kind of evidence derives from the fact that identical mistakes are often committed both by young native learners and by foreign learners of all ages and varying language backgrounds. Such mistakes cover every area of grammatical usage. *He goed there,* is an example of a universal inflectional mistake. *Why he did that?* is an example of a "transformational" error that I have noticed both in the speech of three year old English children and in that of older Indian and Pakistani children at approximately the same stage in learning English. *He is a short,* shows a misuse of the indefinite article that was common to at least one congenitally deaf American child and to an Indian girl whose written style remarkably resembled his. And, finally, the little immigrant, Shanace, did no worse in the "passive" experiment than all but four of the Scottish children of the same age in her Glasgow school.

It is true that there are some mistakes that are peculiar to learners with different mother tongue backgrounds. Most of these are concerned with pronunciation, but they can also affect vocabulary and grammar. In those cases, however, when foreign and native learners make the same mistakes, we can look for a common cause. If the mistakes from both groups of learners also share a common evolutionary history — that is, if they arise at the same learning stage, emerge in the same sequence, and disappear in a similar manner — both kinds of learner may be following the same in-built syllabus, which is only partly affected by methods of teaching and previous knowledge.

The cognitive teacher would accordingly argue:

1. Classroom lessons and language laboratory tapes should be used to determine, largely by the learner's mistakes, where he has got to. We can then give him a push in the right direction. Any number of new structures can be introduced at once to see which ones he can absorb. Different learners may need different experiences and different kinds of problems[8].

The behaviourist teacher, on the other hand, believes:

2. Classroom lessons and language laboratory tapes must both follow a graded external syllabus which introduces one structure at a time in a predetermined order. All students must go through the same syllabus, though their rate of advance may vary.

These contrasting views suggest different images of the language laboratory. In the one case, it is a conveyor belt, like the tape in the machines itself, moving inexorably in a single direction but with different learners perhaps at different points. In the other case, it is more like a library, full of different kinds of books, some difficult, some easy, some informative, some amusing. The learner can be guided to particular sections, but he can also choose for himself. The only thing that all the books have in common is that they are written in the same language.

Both devices, the conveyor belt and the library, appear to have a single objective: to teach the learner the language. But the similarity of aim disappears on closer inspection. The behaviourist approach is intended to teach structures. The cognitive approach is intended to get the learner to induce grammatical rules, together with strategies for their application.

## 11  Structures or rules?

If we enumerated all the sentences derivable from the perfect tense substitution table in Chapter 1, we would have a series of examples of a particular structure. That is, the sentences would be identical in grammatical structure, differing only in the choice of pronouns and vocabulary items:

I have already seen the film.

You have already heard the record.

We have just read the book.

He has just eaten the apple etc.

Some linguists would say that all the sentences reveal the same grammatical pattern. But they only do so to someone who already knows the language. The pattern would not be apparent to a monolingual Navaho Indian, any more than patterns in his language would be apparent to us.

But we can appreciate his woven blankets and he can appreciate our wall-paper. Language patterns are not like visual patterns, obvious to all. They exist only in the trained ear of the hearer.[9]

How then do we know that the set of sentences are identical in structure and display the same pattern? We can only answer this question by saying: it is because they all contain examples of the same grammatical categories (pronoun, adverb, perfect tense forms etc.), and these categories have been arranged in a certain order according to a single set of grammatical rules to the effect that the subject precedes, and the object follows, the verb etc. Knowing the rules, we can recognise the pattern and produce further examples of it. We can follow and apply the rules of our own language even if we have never studied grammar and cannot put them into words.

The learner is in a different position. If we do not tell him what the rules are, he must invent them. In order to recognise the pattern, to master the structure productively, he must make an inductive leap in the dark from example to unknown rule. It is not surprising that he sometimes lands in the wrong place.

## 12  Competence and performance

The learner's inductive task is often described under the two terms *competence* and *performance*.[10] What the learner hears are actual utterances, samples of speech, of somebody else's language performance. If he is to do more than merely parrot these utterances, if he is to understand them and produce similar but differing utterances himself, he must make inferences about the grammatical structure of sentences in the language[11] and the rules that control variations in their structure. When he produces correctly formed novel utterances, we can say that he has learnt part of the language system, or that he has attained a certain competence, or that he now knows the relevant rules — that is, he knows how to deploy them. We speak of his *knowing* the rules, but this is only a metaphor. We cannot observe what is going on in his mind. We can only observe his performance, and conclude from it that he is behaving *as if* he knew the rules.

## 13  Testing the rules

Our test of whether the learner knows a particular rule is whether he can correctly produce an utterance that he has never heard before, and which he cannot therefore be merely copying. This is also the learner's own testing device, and explains once more the importance of making mistakes. When Nasira, a nine year old Pakistani girl, writes: *She is very crying* she is trying to express a bit of information. She is also, however unwittingly, performing a language experiment. The teacher's reaction will inform her that the rules that permit already familiar sentences like *She is very sad, It is very interesting,* cannot be extended to a verb like *cry.* Her teacher could try to show her, by a judicious choice of further examples, that *very* can only be used to intensify adjectives, adverbs of manner and the participles of verbs like *interest, frighten, amuse, tire,* all of which are transitive, and all of which take exclusively animate objects. Of course, the teacher would be very unwise to use these terms, and he might find that Nasira was not yet ready to draw the right inferences from the examples. But if she did appear to understand what was going on, could correct her earlier effort, and produce further correct examples, the teacher might still set her a further test. He might ask her to explain what she was doing.

## 14  To explain or not to explain?

Explanation, in these circumstances, means formulating a rule. It is always possible to know the rule, in the sense of being able to conform with it, without being able to put it into words. What, then, is the point of explanation? The first thing to note, in this connection, is that if no public explanation is given, the learners will very often form their own private explanations. Shanace and her classmates, at the same time as maintaining that

The dog was chased by the cows,

was the same as

The dog chased the cows,

had a perfectly plausible explanation for why the words *was* and *by* occurred in the first sentence. "It's because it's going to be a long story". They were offering a *stylistic* explanation, where we know that a grammatical one is called for.

Ashim, an eight year old Indian boy who had been learning English for only two months, agreed that there was an obvious difference between *car* and *cars*. "You say *car* when it's male, and *cars* when it's female". (He **did** know what the word *car* referred to.) This is a valid type of grammatical explanation, but it is inappropriate.

These two cases illustrate that learners do jump to conclusions. One reason for finding out what these are and for trying to improve on them when they are false, is to prevent unnecessary mistakes in future. A second reason for soliciting explanations obtains when the learner consistently makes a kind of mistake which no amount of drilling can remedy. Let us look at an actual example.

## 15  Jeeto and the verb 'to be'

Jeeto was an immigrant Indian girl, aged twelve, who had been studying at an English school for nine months. She was very keen on writing stories. In one story, fourteen sentences long, occurred the following sentences containing the verb *to be:*

He is a fat.

Today is a very cold.

I'm very sorry.

Your chair is a broken.

Your plate is broken.

He is a sitting on floor.

He is sitting on the chair.

He is a eat a dinner.

Your dinner is fall down.

This is a my story.

I could also add to this list from other children's spoken utterances:

She is a girl.

She is girl.

She is a Shila.

She is Shila.

The most plausible explanation of the apparently random use of the indefinite article, in both legitimate and illegitimate contexts, is that it is intentional. The article is not conceived of as being connected with nouns, but as an optional constituent of the verb *to be*. Jeeto seems to feel that the third person form of this verb is either *is* or *is a*, and both can be used without giving offence. This inference was probably drawn from contrastive drills such as:

This is mother, Peter, Shila, etc.
This is a woman, boy, girl, etc.

Jeeto was perfectly aware of the difference between proper nouns and common nouns. What the drilling failed to make her see was that this was a relevant distinction as far as the occurrence of articles is concerned. Clearly, further drilling of the same kind is not likely to improve matters. What might help is an explanation in terms that she can understand or that she can formulate herself. As Wittgenstein says: "An explanation serves to remove or avert a misunderstanding". It can help the learner "to understand something that is already in plain view".[12]

## 16 Rules and strategies

Jeeto's error, like Shanace's, is to mistake grammatical for stylistic variation. The two are legitimately illustrated in our use of the prepositions *since* and *for*. We can say:

1. I've been waiting for ten minutes.

2. I've been waiting ten minutes.

3. I've been waiting since six o'clock.

but not:

4. I've been waiting six o'clock.

5. I've been waiting for six o'clock (meaning *from* six o'clock).

6. I've been waiting since ten minutes.

Sentences 1 and 2 are stylistic variants. The preposition *for* can be included or omitted according to the inclination of the speaker. Sentence 4 makes it clear that the preposition *since* cannot be omitted. Sentences 5 and 6 reveal the grammatical contrast between *since* and *for*. Although their meaning is similar, they cannot be interchanged. Each is used with a different type of time expression.

Stylistic variants are supposed to be in free variation. But it is very often the case that in certain situations one rather than the other is preferred. It has often been noted, for example, that the passive voice is commonly used in reports of experiments performed by the author himself. To use the active voice is not grammatically wrong; it is stylistically unusual or inappropriate. In extreme cases, the choice of the wrong variant may startle the hearer, as Eliza Dolittle discovered in Shaw's play, *Pygmalion.*

When we ask ourselves what kind of remarks would be appropriate on particular occasions − at an interview, while introducing yourself, when proposing marriage − we cannot often lay down firm rules. In the clearest instances, we are concerned with well-established verbal etiquette; in less clear ones, we have only vague feelings about what the effect of a particular utterance would be. In practice, we seem to follow a number of different verbal strategies, varying our language performance according to the circumstances and the company we are in.

Language learners, as the stories of Shanace and Jeeto show, are aware of the possibility of stylistic variation at an early stage. From the moment they begin to talk, they are faced with choices, both grammatical and stylistic. If only because the two can be so readily confused, the teacher must consider how he can help the learners to distinguish grammatical rules from performance strategies. The words *was* and *by* do not signal the beginning of a long story, but the phrase *once upon a time* does.

## 17 Three questions

In the last six sections we have been looking at a variety of mistakes. We began by enquiring whether mistakes might help a learner to learn. But our study of his mistakes has led us to several questions about what we are trying to teach:

**1. Are we trying to teach structural patterns or rules?** Structural patterns, according to the behaviourist, can be learnt by repetition and drilling. They are a matter for purely mechanical habit formation. But we have seen that despite intensive drilling the learner may fail to see the rule that controls the form and variation of the structure. Perceiving a rule is not a mechanical task. It requires intelligent observation. The cognitive teacher gives the learner experience of the language through listening practice. He tries to direct the learner's observation by setting him problems. Once the rule has been perceived, drills or exercises may well be needed to ensure that the learner learns to apply it.

**2. Should we give or demand explanations?** Explanations need play no part in the behaviourist approach since repetition and drilling can both be undertaken without them. But they cannot be so easily dispensed with if the learner persists in making mistakes through having failed to infer a rule correctly. In the cognitive approach the function of an explanation is to help the learner organise his experience by putting his observations into words.

**3. Should we teach performance strategies as well as grammar?** Some of the mistakes we looked at suggested that we are not just concerned with getting the learner to perceive a rule or to master a structure. We must also train him when to use this structure and when not to. Otherwise he may say things that are perfectly correct grammatically but situationally inappropriate. To develop appropriate performance strategies we need something more sophisticated than the structural drill. This is the domain of role-playing exercises and games.

In this chapter, we have explored two different attitudes to mistakes and two differing concepts of the syllabus. I have sketched the function of repetition and drilling in the behaviourist approach, and of listening practice, problems and exercises in the cognitive. The two approaches offer contrasting views of the best way of using the language laboratory. In our own laboratories, we must either choose between these views, or reconcile them. We may feel more inclined to try one approach rather than the other. But if the approach we adopt produces good results, it does not mean that we need look no further. The other might have proved still more effective. We can only reject a possibility when we have found it does not work.

Subsequent chapters provide examples of each form of practice that the reader can put to the test in his own laboratory. But first I would like to give him the experience of some of the forms of practice himself. The only way I can do this is by giving a lesson in a new language.

# Novish—An experiment in language learning

1.    I am going to teach you something of a new language called Novish. It might be described as a creole language since much of its vocabulary is obviously derived from English. There is no need for me, therefore, to translate the vocabulary items, but I will ask you some questions about the structure of various sentences. If this experiment is to work, I would like you to try to answer the questions before you look at the answer in the frame below.

2.    Here are some pictures of common objects and this is what a Novish speaker might say:

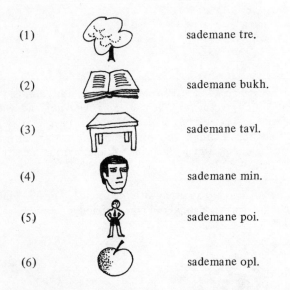

(1)     sademane tre.

(2)     sademane bukh.

(3)     sademane tavl.

(4)     sademane min.

(5)     sademane poi.

(6)     sademane opl.

Without worrying about how the words would be pronounced, it is fairly easy to recognise the names of the different objects. But what do you think the phrase *sademane* means?

3.    If you think that *sademane* means something like *This is a ...*, you will be on fairly safe ground for the moment. Of course, you can't yet tell whether it consists of one word or more than one word, and it is impossible to judge whether Novish has an article system like English. But notice what happens to *sademane* in the next few examples:

(7)                    sademanena gal.

(8)          sademanena ku.

(9)          sademanena kot.

Now what conditions govern the ending *na,* which occurred in the last three examples? Would you for instance, use *sademane* or *sademanena* in the next example?

(10)                    ....................................weimin.

4.    The correct answer would be: *sademane weimin.* In other words, the word *weimin* is not preceded by the ending *na.* Why not, and when should this ending be used? If you look at examples 7–9 again (which do take this ending), you may notice that they all have something in common, which distinguishes them from the other nouns used so far. What is it?

5.    The words *gal, ku,* and *kot* all begin with the sound /k/ or /g/. Which ending would you now use to precede the compound noun *kupoi* in this example?

(11)                    ....................................kupoi.

6.    You should have said: *sademanena kupoi* as the ending *na* must always occur before a word beginning with /k/ or /g/. It relates, in other words, to this particular phonological feature and not to any system of gender, such as you would find in Latin or French. You now know how to make simple statements in Novish. Now look at the following pictures and what is being said about them:

(12)      Ki tavl sademane?
Ye sadestil tavl.

(13)      Ki bukh sademane?
Ye sadestil bukh.

(14)      Ki hus sademane?
Ye sadestil hus.

You will have noticed the question mark in the first of each pair of sentences and the different word order in the questions. What do you think the word *ki* means?

7.   For the time being, you can assume that *ki* is some kind of question marker. In other words, the question

     Ki hus sademane?

might be translated into English as:

     ...............................................?

8.   So you are being asked something like,

     Is this a house?

and if the picture shows a house, you must reply in Novish with:

     ...............................................

9.   You will have noticed that, in answer to this question, Novish speakers do not say:

     Ye sademane hus

but

     Ye sadestil hus

But this new ending still is not found in answer to all questions. Look at the next examples:

(15)      Ki poi sademane?
Ye sadegru poi.

(16)      Ki weimin sademane?
Ye sadegru weimin.

(17)      Ki min sademane?
Ye sadegru min.

How would you answer the next question?

(18)            Ki gal sademane?

Ye ..................................... gal.

10.    The right answer is,

Ye sadegru gal.

How would you answer this question:

(19)            Ki tren sademane?

Ye ..................................... tren.

11.    The right answer is

Ye sadestil tren.

If you have got both the last questions right, you may have obtained some idea of the difference between *sadegru* and *sadestil*. To see how right you are, answer this question:

(20)            Ki opl sademane?

Ye ..................................... opl.

12.    The answer is

Ye sadegru opl

and if you got it wrong, you must try to think what apples and people have in common which is not shared by trains and tables etc.

13.    Apples and people *grow*, and the distinction between things that grow and things that don't is very important in Novish when you are answering questions. If you look back at examples 12–20, you can see that the phrase *sadegru* is always used in answer to questions about growing things, and the phrase *sadestil* in answer to questions about non-growing things. Somewhat misleading from our point of view, is the use of the word *stil* (still) with moving but ungrowing objects such as trains. Now have a look at the following examples:

(21)           Ki poi sademane?

Nu sadegru poi, sadestil tavl!

(22)           Ki weimin sademane?

Nu sadegru weimin, sadestil bukh!

(23)   Ki tavl sademane?
Nu sadestil tavl, sadegru poi!

(24)  Ki hus sademane?
Nu sadestil hus, sadegru ku!

You will have noticed that the words *sadegru* and *sadestil* are still occurring regularly with growing and non-growing objects respectively but instead of each answer beginning with the word *Ye* as in examples 12–20, it now begins with the word *Nu*. What do you think these two words mean?

14. If you think they mean approximately the same as the English words *Yes* and *No* (or affirmative and negative), how would you answer these questions?

(25)  Ki hus sademane?
.................... sadestil hus.

(26)  Ki gal sademane?
.................... sadegru gal, sadestil hus!

15. So far, so good: the first answer should contain *Ye* and the second *Nu*. What about these two questions?

(27)  Ki bukh sademane?
........... sadestil bukh, sadestil tavl!

(28)  Ki weimin sademane?
........... sadegru weimin, sadegru ku!

16. In answering both the last two questions, the word *Ye* should be used, and not the word *Nu*. Why? What then determines the use of *Ye* and *Nu*, if it is not simple confirmation or negation of a *Yes/No* question? I could show you many more examples of the usage of the two words in Novish, but it is probably quicker to explain by means of translation. I allowed you to think – and indeed without translation I would have no means of preventing you from thinking – that the simple statement in Novish *sademane poi* corresponds to the English *This is a boy*. It does to a certain extent, and the one is the normal equivalent of the other in most situations, but a more careful translation of the Novish would render it in English as

This object belongs to the class of boys.

The Novish question form:

Ki poi sademane?

would then correspond more closely to an English rendering:

Does this object belong to the class of boys?

If it does, we agree with the questioner and say:

Yes, it grows like a boy (Ye sadegru poi).

Remember that in answering this kind of question we must always specify whether the object we are talking about grows or not. If the questioner points to a girl and asks whether she has the properties of a boy, in Novish we must still agree with him about the essential property of growing, but point out his error of subclassification. So the correct answer in this situation would be:

Yes, it grows like a girl, (but) it is a boy.
Ye sadegru gal, sadegru poi!

Only when the questioner mistakes a growing object for a non-growing object will the polite Novish speaker contradict him fully:

Does this object belong to the class of boys?
No, it doesn't grow like a boy, it is still like a book.
(Nu sadegru poi, sadestil bukh!)

17.    Remember that the problems you have encountered in Novish are not unlike some of those that foreign learners have to face in English. The distinction between *sademane* and *sademanena* resembles that between the two forms of the indefinite article, *a* and *an*. The grammatical difference between *gru* and *stil* nouns has as much natural logic, and as much inconsistency in its application, as the English contrast between countable and uncountable nouns, or the French contrast between masculine and feminine genders. The strange business of how to answer questions in the negative reflects the difficulties that Poles, Japanese, and speakers of many African languages have in answering English questions like:

Isn't it raining?

Won't you have another cup of tea?

I'm a fool, aren't I?

If you are aggrieved, rather than amused, by your failure to get everything right first time, remember that young Novish children make the same mistakes, and that I was going out of my way to trap you. I wanted to establish the validity of a number of points touched upon in the last chapter:

**1. You can get some things right for the wrong reasons.** You may just be guessing, or you may have completely misunderstood the rules of the language. Mere production of the "right" response, even on a number of occasions, does not necessarily indicate successful learning.

**2. You can get some things wrong without knowing why.** Looking at the right answer will not necessarily help you. This suggests that we should treat with some caution the language laboratory teacher's claim to give his pupils immediate *knowledge* of results in the form of the right answer on the tape. It would be safer to say that he only *acquaints* the pupil with the right answer. The pupil may not know why it is right or whether he is wrong.

**3. You can get things wrong at the same time as being aware of what is right.** This possibility suggests that we should approach mistakes as cautiously as we must approach apparently right answers. Mistakes may be due only to carelessness. They may represent slips of the tongue or memory which are common enough even in the speech of native speakers. Knowing the rule, in the sense of being able to formulate it, is no guarantee that we will consistently be able to apply it. Accommodation must be followed by never-ending practice at assimilation.

**4. Whether you get things right, or whether you get things wrong, you cannot proceed very far in a language without attempting to form explanations.** Language learning is not just a mechanical business of trial and error. At certain points, it involves either reasoning or intuition, together with a knowledge of the world. (Think how valuable for learning Novish it is to know already which things grow and which things don't.) This is why machines can never learn languages — though they can be programmed to perform as if they knew them — and why it is unwise to treat the learner as if he were a machine. There is a risk that he might behave like one!

With these principles in mind, we can now begin to study the different forms of practice that we could test on our own pupils.

NOTES

1. "We lie more than we need for lack of imagination: the truth is also invented."
2. "Speech does not permit of being taught, but only of being awoken in the mind."
3. The labels "cognitive" and "behaviourist" reflect the differing emphases of the two schools. A behaviourist, such as Skinner, claims to be concerned exclusively with describing, and preferably measuring, the observable behaviour of his subjects, human and animal. Cognitive psychologists, such as Piaget and Vygotsky, are concerned with inferring, from their subjects' observable behaviour, the nature and development of their mental "equipment" and cognitive processes. For their differing views on language learning, see B. F. Skinner: *Verbal Behaviour,* Appleton, Century, Crofts, 1957; J. Piaget: *The Language and*

*Thought of the Child,* reprinted by Meridian Bocks, 1955; L. S. Vygotsky: *Thought and Language,* M.I.T. Press, 1962.

4. For a thorough investigation and criticism of these criteria of grading, see H. G. Widdowson: "The Teaching of English through Science", in *Language in Education,* Oxford University Press, 1968.
5. See for example the illustration of teaching by involvement in Chapter 1, section 5. For a fuller account of this kind of teaching, see J. and F. Stoddart: *The Teaching of English to Immigrant Children,* University of London Press, 1968.
6. See also H. G. Widdowson: "The Teaching of English through Science", Chapters 4 and 5, op. cit., for a proposed cognitive syllabus for secondary school pupils in India and Pakistan.
7. Conducted and reported by D. R. Bradley in *An Investigation of Reading,* op. cit.
8. For a fuller description of a learner-controlled syllabus, see R. F. Mager: "On the Sequencing of Instructional Content", *Psychological Reports* (405–412), 1961.
9. For a fuller discussion of this point, see J. P. Thorne: "On Hearing Sentences", in *Psycholinguistics Papers,* ed. Lyons and Wales, Edinburgh University Press, 1966.
10. There is a fuller discussion of these terms in *Psycholinguistics Papers,* cited above.
11. For a meticulous distinction between the terms *utterance* and *sentence,* see J. Lyons: *Introduction to Theoretical Linguistics,* Cambridge University Press, 1968.
12. *Philosophical Investigations,* Blackwell, 1958.

# 3 Listening practice

*He that hath ears to hear,*
*let him hear.*

THE GOSPEL OF ST. MARK

## 1 Listening and hearing

In Chapter 2, Section 4, I drew a distinction between *hearing* someone talking in a language that we do not know, and *listening* to someone talking a language that we do. Listening is one half of the process of communication. It presupposes in the hearer a willingness and a competence to understand what is said. In the behaviourist classroom and language laboratory, listening is a rare event. Apart from interpreting spoken instructions, the learner uses his ears only for the purpose of hearing: hearing examples of the new structure, hearing cues for his own responses, hearing the correct response afterwards. He does not need to understand what the examples or the responses mean. Indeed, since they are only examples of what could be said, rather than utterances relating to a particular situation, they are not intended to mean anything. I do not imply that they are always nonsensical, just that they convey no information.

The behaviourist teacher is understandably wary of getting his pupils to listen. The communication of novel information — by means of conversation, exposition or narrative — often involves the use of structures and vocabulary that will not yet be familiar to the learners. Such a haphazard introduction of new items plays havoc with his graded syllabus, and may lead to confusion in the minds of the learners. The behaviourist would prefer that what the learners hear was at the most only one structure in advance of what they can produce. This places second language learning in complete contrast with performance in the mother tongue. In the latter we hear and understand a great many words, structures, and stylistic devices that we have never ourselves used. But if we hear them often enough, and the need for them arises, we may find ourselves using them without having consciously learnt them. This observation leads the cognitive teacher to regard listening as potentially an equally effective means of presentation and practice in the second language.

## 2 Listening as a means of presentation

In the same class of beginners as Jeeto, there was a nine year old Italian boy called Joseph who could not get the present continuous tense right either. One day when he was asked where Jeeto was, instead of producing his usual

She is a swim,

he said:
> She might have gone swimming.

He must have picked this structure up from watching television or from something his teacher may once have said unreflectingly. Unlike the present continuous tense, it was recalled correctly and effortlessly without any repetition or drilling. This story reveals that structures and vocabulary can sometimes be learnt quite independently of the teacher and his syllabus, simply by listening to people talking. If we want to give the learner the opportunity of learning on his own, as the language laboratory enables us to do, we should give him a great deal of simple and interesting material to listen to. The published courses that most fully put this principle into practice are the "old-fashioned" Assimil books. For the first 50–60 lessons, the learner does nothing but listen to records containing conversations, following them in the book if he wishes. Understanding is ensured by the provision of a written translation,[1] and tested by a whole series of jokes. Apart from laughter, no further overt response is required. The learner is given the chance of learning, as the title of each Assimil course promises, "without toil"

## 3  Listening as a means of practice

As a means of presentation, listening teaches by involvement. As a means of practice, it aids remembering by repetition. The same story or conversation can be listened to by the learner as many times as he wishes. The repetition can also take a less obvious form within each story, or from conversation to conversation. Each lesson, for example, of the Harcourt, Brace and World courses mentioned in Chapter 1 contains a "basic dialogue". To help the learner remember its content he hears as many as eight or nine supplementary conversations in the course of the lesson unit employing similar language in different situations.

Repetition within a story can take two forms. Children's fairy stories like "Goldilocks and the Three Bears" employ cyclic repetition. The same episodes are repeated, but with new participants. Songs like "Ten Men Went to Mow", or "The Twelve Days of Christmas" , most aptly illustrate cumulative repetition. The same language is repeated, but something new is added each time. Both techniques are employed in the sample listening materials at the end of this chapter.

Repetition facilitates remembering. It does not ensure understanding. I will discuss techniques of promoting understanding in the chapter on the design of comprehension exercises. But, even anticipating a successful solution of this problem, there are other questions about the designing and grading of listening materials still unasked and unanswered. What sort of language, for instance, should we get the learner to listen to? Let us look first at what we should not make him listen to.

Rumpelstiltskin.

## 4 The case of the amnesiac siblings

There once came into my hands the manuscript of a proposed primary school course for foreign learners. The course was described by the author as being structural, situational, contextual, and logical. Each lesson began with a short conversation between two English children. In the first conversation, they find out each other's names by the simple expedient of asking:

What is your name?

When they next meet in Lesson 2, having meanwhile forgotten, they play the Rumpelstiltskin game:

Is your name John? *No, it isn't.*

Is your name Henry? *No, it isn't.*

Is your name Sebastian? etc.

Failing to guess aright, they eventually resort to the direct question form of Lesson 1. In Lesson 3, they have both again been overcome by a loss of memory. They repeat the guessing game until some dim stirring of recollection prompts the right suggestion, and the gratifying answer: "Yes, it is". In Lessons 4 and 5, they change the subject. The conversation runs on the following lines:

Is that a bag? *Yes, it is.*

Is it a book? *No, it isn't.*

Is it a table? *No, it isn't.*

What is it? *It's a bag.*

In Lesson 6, it turns out that the boy and the girl are brother and sister.

## 5 Structurespeech

The children in the previous section don't talk, they *structurespeak*. This term describes the process of speaking like a structural drill. Notice that their structurespeech conveys no information, or at least none that they do not already know, such as each other's names, and the names of common objects. Perhaps this is why they never appear to listen to what is being said. I have reported their conversations at length only because, if this is the kind of language we present to our pupils in the language laboratory, there is a considerable risk that they will not listen either. The word *practice* does not have the same meaning when we conjoin it to words like *listening* and *speech*. We can practise speaking, or rather structurespeech, quite meaninglessly — as we shall see in the next chapter. But we cannot practise listening meaninglessly. Either the learner is listening to something he understands at least in part, to something that imparts information or elicits laughter, or, alternatively, he is just hearing that something is being said, something that has no why or wherefore.

## 6  Conversation and spoken prose

The two children also speak in *spoken prose*. Theirs happens to be highly implausible, but any conversation which has been scripted in advance is a sample of spoken prose. It is not a sample of *conversation*.[2] There is a world of difference — phonetic, phonological, grammatical and stylistic — between the scripted, rehearsed dialogue of the stage or of the tape-recorded course,[3] and what we hear around us every day. It is true that we may wish to train our students to appreciate dramatic dialogue, but we should not forget to equip them for taking part in genuine conversation. They can listen to what we say in the classroom, but apart from this the language laboratory offers them the only leisurely opportunity they will have of listening to how native speakers actually talk. Listening to spoken prose may be a preparation for this. It is not a sufficient substitute.

## 7  The value of the laboratory as a listening device

In the past the laboratory has been used principally as a means of getting the learner to talk. It has been rather neglected as a means of getting him to listen. Yet this is one area, and perhaps the only one, in which the laboratory is unquestionably more effective than the classroom. In the laboratory the learner can hear a variety of voices and accents apart from the teacher's. He can listen to what people actually say in situations that can only be simulated in the classroom. He can listen to each story of conversation as many times as he wishes. And, provided there is a sufficient range of materials, he can choose materials that suit his own interests and level of understanding.

The question, to my mind, is not whether to use the laboratory for listening practice, but how to do so most effectively. Ultimately we may want our pupils to be able to listen to and learn from actual conversation. But to begin with we might be wiser to use spoken prose. If, for example, we write and record our own listening materials, we can control both their structure and their content. Controlling their content means ensuring that the language is not too difficult for a particular learner, that it does not contain unnecessary problems of style, vocabulary or grammatical usage. Controlling the structure of listening materials means ensuring that the meaning of new items can be inferred from the context. It may also mean helping the learner to remember the new items through the skilful use of repetition. Children's rhymes and stories, as we have already noted, suggest several ways of employing repetition without losing the attention of the listener. They also remind us of the importance of making listening materials interesting or enjoyable. The problem is to involve the learner in listening. He will learn nothing if he is bored, however carefully controlled our materials may be.

The three listening passages that follow are attempts to make listening worthwhile. They are all stories originally composed for children, though they have also been used with adults. They might first be presented to the learners orally in class with some kind of visual accompaniment such as flannelgraph figures. The learners who like them can then be encouraged to listen to them again in the laboratory. At some subsequent stage, the same stories might be presented again in a third form, in writing, for reading practice.

The three stories are extracted from a sequence of more than a hundred, some of which were presented to the learners in their first year of learning English. The first example came fairly early in the sequence. The story-line is simple and a heavy use is made of cyclic repetition. This lightens the load on the learner's understanding at the same time as helping to familiarise him with the vocabulary and structures employed. If the story has any particular teaching point, it is the names of verbs of action such as *run, walk, dance, sing* etc. and the use of the present tenses. But the learners may pick up things from the story which we were scarcely aware of teaching. One class, for example, was particularly struck by the negative request, *"Please don't eat me"!* and this form appeared spontaneously in their conversation soon after hearing the story.

## 8 'Mr. Tiger is sleeping' — a listening passage

"Grrrr!"

Who is this? Yes, it's a tiger. It is a big, orange and black tiger. He is sleepy. He is very sleepy. So he shuts one eye slowly. Then he shuts both eyes slowly. Now he is sleeping. He is sleeping under a tree. He is sleeping under a big, green banana tree.

"Caw. Caw."

Who is this? Yes, it's a crow. It's an old crow. It's an old black crow. He can see the tiger. He can see the tiger sleeping under the big, green banana tree. The crow begins to laugh. Then he begins to sing. He sings a little song:

"One, two, three,
What can I see?
A big, fat tiger
Sleeping under a tree."

The crow sings a little song. Then he begins to dance.

"I'm walking, I'm walking, I'm walking.
I'm skipping, I'm skipping, I'm skipping.
I'm jumping, I'm jumping, I'm jumping.
Mr. Tiger is sleeping.
He can't catch me."

And the crow begins to walk and skip and jump.

"Eee, Eee."

Who is this? Yes, it's a rat. It is a fat, black rat. The rat says:

"What are you doing, Mr. Crow?"

The crow says:

"Look. The tiger is sleeping under the green banana tree. So I'm singing and I'm dancing."

"Oh," says the rat. "Oh. Then I will sing and dance too." And the rat begins to laugh. The rat and the crow both begin to laugh. Then the rat and the crow both begin to sing. They both begin to sing a little song:

"One, two, three,
What can we see?
A big, fat tiger
Sleeping under a tree."

The rat and the crow both sing the song. Then they both begin to dance.

"We're walking, we're walking, we're walking.
We're skipping, we're skipping, we're skipping.
We're jumping, we're jumping, we're jumping.
Mr. Tiger is sleeping.
He can't catch me."

And the rat and the crow both begin to walk and skip and jump and dance under the green banana tree.

"Cluck, Cluck, Cluck."

Who is this? Yes, it's a hen. It is a little red hen. The hen says:

"What are you doing, Mr. Rat and Mr. Crow?"

The rat and the crow both say:

"Look. The tiger is sleeping under the green banana tree. So we are singing and dancing."

"Oh," says the hen. "Oh. Then I will sing and dance too."

And the hen and the rat and the crow begin to laugh. They all begin to laugh. Then the hen and the rat and the crow begin to laugh. They all begin to laugh. Then the hen and the rat and the crow begin to sing. They all begin to sing a little song:

"One, two, three,
What can we see?
A big, fat tiger
Sleeping under a tree."

The hen and the rat and the crow sing the song. Then they all begin to dance:

"We're walking, we're walking, we're walking.
We're skipping, we're skipping, we're skipping.
We're jumping, we're jumping, we're jumping.

Mr. Tiger is sleeping.
He can't catch me."

And the hen and the rat and the crow begin to walk and skip and jump and dance under the green banana tree. The tiger opens one eye. The tiger opens both eyes. He has got big, yellow eyes and a very big, red mouth. He opens his mouth. He has got very big, white teeth.

"Quick, quick," says Mr. Crow. "Jump into the tree."
"Quick, quick," says Mr. Rat. "Jump into the tree."
"Quick, quick," says Mrs. Hen. "Jump into the tree".

And they all jump into the tree very quickly. The tiger stands up. He stands up slowly. And he laughs. He looks at the crow and the rat and the hen, and he begins to laugh. Then the tiger begins to sing. He sings a little song:

"One, two, three
What can I see?
A crow, a rat and a hen
Sitting in a tree."

The crow says: "Good morning, Mr. Tiger. Please don't eat me."
The rat says: "Good morning, Mr. Tiger. Please don't eat me."
The hen says: "Good morning, Mr. Tiger. Please don't eat me."
The tiger begins to laugh. Then he says:

"Mmmmmmmm I will eat you. I am hungry. I am very hungry. I will eat you. I will eat you all for breakfast."

And, very quickly the tiger jumps into the tree. But the tiger does not catch the crow. The crow can fly. The crow quickly flies up into the sky. And the tiger does not catch the hen. The hen can fly too. The hen quickly flies up into the sky. And the tiger doesn't catch the rat. The rat can't fly. But he is very small. And he jumps into a hole. He jumps into a very small hole in the green banana tree.

So the tiger doesn't eat the crow or the hen or the rat for breakfast. He doesn't eat any breakfast that day. So he shuts one eye slowly. Then he shuts both eyes slowly. And he goes to sleep again under the green banana tree.

Then the crow and the rat and the hen begin to sing again. They all begin to sing:

"One, two, three,
What can we see?
A big, fat tiger
Sleeping under a tree.
Silly old tiger,
You can't catch me."

## 9 'Shila and the Witch' — a listening passage

Shila's father has three goats and one little white sheep.

One day Shila's father said to Shila:

"Shila, I want you to look after the little white sheep today. Find some green grass for him to eat. And mind you don't lose him."

So Shila took the little white sheep and she began to look for some green grass. At last she found some long, green grass, and the little white sheep began to eat.

"Baa, baa," he said.

It was a very hot day. The sun was shining high in the sky. It was so hot that Shila began to feel sleepy. She sat down under a green banana tree.

"Oh dear," she said. "It is so hot, and I am so sleepy. I must shut my eyes just for one minute. Just for one minute. Now, mind you don't run away, little white sheep!"

And Shila shut her eyes and fell fast asleep.

But she did not sleep for just one minute. She slept for one, two, three, four hours. When she woke up and opened her eyes, the sun was low in the sky. It was getting cold and dark.

"Oh dear," said Shila, "I slept for a long time. Now I must go home with the little white sheep."

And she began to look for the little white sheep. But she could not see him anywhere.

"Little white sheep, little white sheep, where are you?" she called.

"Come back, oh please come back, or my father will be very angry."

She looked here; she looked there; she looked everywhere, but she couldn't see the little white sheep. She listened here; she listened there; she listened everywhere, but she couldn't hear the little white sheep.

"Oh dear," she said, "I must find him. I can't go home until I find him or my father will be very angry."

So she walked and she looked and she listened and she sang a little song:

"A, B, C, D, E, F, G,
My sheep is hiding far from me.
Looking here, looking there
I can't see him anywhere."

And she stopped to call:

"Little white sheep, little white sheep, where are you? Come back, oh please come back, or my father will be very angry."

But the little white sheep did not come back. And she couldn't see him anywhere.

So she walked and she looked and she listened and she sang another little song about another little girl who had lost some sheep:

"Little Bo-peep has lost her sheep
And doesn't know where to find them.
Leave them alone, and they will come home
Bringing their tails behind them."

And she stopped to call:

"Little white sheep, little white sheep, where are you? Come home, oh please come home, or my father will be very angry."

But the little white sheep did not come back. And she couldn't see him anywhere.

So Shila walked and she looked and she listened until at last she came to a little house made of sticks. Sitting outside the house was a big fat orange cat.

"Pussy, oh Pussy," said Shila, "can you help me? I went to sleep and lost my sheep, and I don't know where to find him. Have you seen my little white sheep anywhere?"

"Miaow," said the orange cat. "Go away, little girl. Go away quickly. This is the house of a wicked witch. If she finds you here, she will turn you into a green frog."

"But I can't go home," said Shila, "until I find my little white sheep or my father will be very angry."

And just then she heard the little sheep say "Baa!" The little sheep was inside the house of the wicked witch!

Shila was very frightened but she knocked at the door: rat a tat tat.

From inside the house came a voice, a very horrible voice:

"Who is that?"

"It is only a little girl. I went to sleep and lost my sheep and I don't know where to find him. Have you seen my little white sheep?"

The door of the little house opened and out came a wicked witch.

She had a horrible, green face, and horrible, green hands, and horrible, yellow eyes, and horrible, long, yellow teeth. On her head was a very long, blue hat.

She gave Shila a horrible smile.

"So you have lost your sheep, have you, little girl? You went to sleep and lost your sheep."

And the witch laughed a horrible laugh.

"Well, I have found your little white sheep. And I am going to eat him. I am going to eat him for my dinner."

"Oh no," said Shila, "please don't eat my little white sheep or my father will be very angry with me."

"Yes," said the witch, "I will eat your sheep and I will turn you into a green frog."

"Oh no," said Shila. "Please don't do that. Please don't turn me into a green frog. I will be a very good girl and do anything you say."

"Well, well, well," said the witch. "Well, perhaps I won't turn you into a green frog........just yet. But you must clean the house for me tomorrow. Now come inside and go to sleep."

And the witch pulled Shila inside the house and shut the door.

Shila had to sleep on the floor. She did not sleep very well. She was very frightened.

The next morning, the witch woke her up.

"Get up, get up. Get out of bed, you sleepy head. It is time to clean the house. I am going away all day. Mind the house is clean when I come back, or I will turn you into a green frog."

Then the witch picked up her magic broomstick. She pointed her fingers at the broom, and she said:

"Abracadabra wizzy woo,

I can fly and so can you!"

Then she sat on the broomstick and

WHOOSH!

she flew up high into the sky and over the trees.

When the witch had gone, Shila began to cry.

"Oh dear, what shall I do? I don't want to be a green frog."

"Miaow," said the orange cat. "Don't cry, little girl. If you clean the house, the witch won't turn you into a green frog."

"But how shall I clean the house?" said Shila.

"That's easy," said Pussy.

"Wash the windows.

Polish the door.

Clean the table

And sweep the floor."

"But how can I sweep the floor?" said Shila. "The witch has taken away the broomstick."

"That's easy," said Pussy. "I will sweep the floor with my long, bushy tail. You wash the windows, clean the table and polish the door."

So the cat began to sweep the floor with his long bushy tail.

Shila began to wash the windows.

Then she began to polish the door.

Then she began to clean the table.

At last everything was clean. And just then

WHOOSH!

the witch was back, flying on her magic broomstick.

"Is the house clean?" she said.

"Yes," said Shila, "everything is clean.

I have washed the windows.

I have polished the door.

I have cleaned the table

And swept the floor."

"Yes, yes," said the witch. "I can see that. But have you cooked the dinner?"

"No," said Shila. "I haven't cooked the dinner. There isn't anything to eat."

"Yes, there is," said the witch. "There is your little white sheep.

Put some water in a pot.

Make it nice and hot.

Then pop the sheep into the pot

And I will eat the lot.

So you put some water in a pot quickly or I will turn you into a green frog."

"Oh Pussy," said Shila, "What shall I do? The witch wants to eat my little white sheep. If I don't put the sheep into the pot, she will turn me into a green frog. And I don't want to be a green frog."

"Miaow," said the orange cat. "Why don't you turn *her* into a green frog?"

"But how can I turn her into a green frog?" said Shila.

"That's easy," said Pussy. "You point your fingers at the witch and you say:

"Abracadabra wizzy wog
I will turn you into a frog!"

"Thank you, Pussy," said Shila.

"What are you two talking about?" said the witch. "Have you made the water hot? Have you put the sheep in the pot?"

"No," said Shila, "And I am not going to."

"What?" said the witch. "Do you want me to turn you into a green frog?"

"No," said Shila, "And you are not going to. I am going to turn *you* into a green frog!"

And quickly Shila pointed her fingers at the witch and said:

"Abracadabra wizzy wog
I will turn you into a frog!"

And

WHISH! the witch turned into a green frog.

"Brek a kek kek koax koax," she said.

"Thank you again, Pussy," said Shila. "Now I can go home with my little white sheep. Would you like to come to my home with me?"

"Miaow," said Pussy. "Will you give me milk to drink and fish to eat every day?"

"Yes, Pussy," said Shila. "You shall have milk for breakfast and fish for lunch and meat for dinner."

"Well," said Pussy, "let's go to your house quickly because it is time for dinner and I would like some meat to eat. Let's take the witch's magic broomstick."

So Shila pointed her fingers at the magic broomstick and said:

"Abracadabra wizzy woo
I can fly and so can you!"

Then she picked up the little white sheep and sat on the broomstick. Pussy sat down behind her.

And

WHOOSH! they flew up high into the sky.

"Goodbye, wicked witch," said Shila.

"Brek a kek kek koax koax," said the frog.

## 10  'The Star Lady' — a listening passage

Shila was singing a song:

"Ride a cockhorse to Banbury Cross.
See a fine lady upon a white horse.
Rings on her fingers and bells on her toes,
She shall have music wherever she goes."

"Mr. Crow," asked Neal, "who was the lady upon the white horse?"

"Ah," said Mr. Crow, "that means a story. Are you sure you don't want to read your books, or to draw a picture?"

"No," said Shila and Neal. "We want the story."

"Well," said Mr. Crow, "once upon a time there was a boy."

"What was his name?" asked Neal.

"His name was Thomas," said Mr. Crow. "And he didn't believe in fairies. Do you believe in fairies?"

"No," said Neal.

"Sometimes," said Shila.

"Well," said Mr. Crow, "Thomas said he didn't believe in them at all. He lived with his aunt and she had told him there weren't any fairies. But Thomas still liked fairy stories and he used to tell stories himself about what he did. He had a cockhorse. Do you know what a cockhorse is?"

"No," said Neal.

"I think I do," said Shila.

"It's a wooden stick," said Mr. Crow, "with a horse's head. You can ride it." Thomas said his cockhorse was a real horse. He said it could talk and it could run by itself. His aunt didn't believe him.

One day, Thomas said to his cockhorse: "Let's go for a ride."

"It's too late for a ride," said the cockhorse. "You should be going to bed."

"I don't want to go to bed," said Thomas. "I want to go for a ride. Just a short one."

But it was not a short ride.

They went on and on until they came to Banbury Cross. Now in those days — and this was long ago — Banbury Cross was a big, grey stone cross standing all alone in a wood. It had strange pictures on it. There were pictures of the stars and of the moon. And there was a picture of people riding in and out of a round hill.

When Thomas and the cockhorse got to the cross, the sun was setting. Long shadows were growing under the trees and a red moon had just come up.

"We should be at home," said the cockhorse, "it's getting dark."

"I'm not afraid of the dark," said Thomas.

"But it's midsummer night," said the cockhorse.

"What's midsummer night?" asked Thomas.

"It's the night of the 24th of June, the longest day in the year. It's the night when the fairies come out."

"There aren't any fairies," said Thomas.

Just then they heard someone singing. It was a strange song and Thomas didn't understand it. Perhaps the cockhorse did, because he said:

"Let's go now, before it is too late."

But it was too late already. Something white was coming up the path. They could not go back. There was a strange sound:

Clip jingle tingle clop,
Clippety tinklety clop.

"Do you think it is a ghost?" asked Thomas.

The white thing got bigger and the strange sound got louder until ........

"It's a great white horse," said Thomas.

"And there's somebody on it," said the cockhorse.

"Yes," said Mr. Crow. It was a fine lady. She really did have rings on her fingers and bells on her toes. The bells were making the strange sound when the horse walked. She also had a harp in her hand. She was playing it softly while she was singing to herself.

She looked very fine to Thomas for her dress was made of silver and there was starlight in her hair. When she was near, she stopped singing. She looked at Thomas for a long time, and then she smiled.

"You have ridden far to see me," she said.

"Yes," said Thomas. "I mean no. I mean I have come a long way from my home, but I didn't know I would see you. Is this your house?"

The lady smiled again. "My house is near here," she said. "Would you like to see it?"

Thomas did not know what to say.

"It has a ceiling of stars," the lady said, "and they will sing you to sleep."

"I don't want to sleep, thank you," said Thomas. "But are there any cakes and are there any toys?"

"I don't know what toys are," said the lady.

"My horse is a toy," said Thomas.

"No, I'm not," said the cockhorse.

"But I have some cakes," said the lady. "They are spiced with the finest spells. You can eat them all night and never get sick."

"I'm very hungry," said Thomas. "I would like to eat one of your cakes."

"Come to my house, then," said the lady.

"Don't go," said the cockhorse, "and don't eat anything."

"Your own horse is tired," said the lady. "Come up and ride with me on mine."

Thomas jumped up on the great white horse. The little cockhorse jumped up too. The lady had not asked him, but he was not going to be left behind.

How high it was from the ground! Thomas looked down again. It was too high. The ground was far below.

"We are flying!" he said.

"No," said the lady. "We are standing quite still."

Thomas looked down again. It was true. The great white horse was still but the ground was moving slowly beneath them. A round green hill was coming nearer. There was a great black hole in the side of the hill like the mouth of a cave.

"There are stars inside that hill," said Thomas.

"There are stars inside every hill if you know how to see them," said the lady. "That hill is my home."

The mouth of the hill grew bigger and blacker and the stars inside shone brighter. There was a sound of strange singing and suddenly they were inside. Thomas could not see outside any more. The sky was all black and full of stars. The stars were big and clean and flickering strangely.

"The stars are singing!" said Thomas.

"Yes," said the lady. "Every star sings if you know how to listen. Did you not hear me singing just now?"

"You have got a moon in here too," said Thomas. "But it's the wrong colour. It's blue and white and it's too big."

"Our moon has clouds and water on it," said the lady. "Those are the colours that you can see."

"And there's something brown, too," said Thomas.

"That's the land where the people live," said the lady.

"Oh," said Thomas. "I would like to go to that moon. What are the moon people like?"

"Just like you," said the lady.

"Can I have a cake now?" asked Thomas.

The cakes were shaped like stars. They were thin and shiny but they were good to eat. Thomas ate one slowly. Then he ate another one quickly. Then he ate two more when the lady was not looking. Soon the plate was finished.

"I think I shall go home now," said Thomas.

"I will sing to you," said the lady.

She picked up her harp and began to sing softly. Thomas began to feel sleepy.

"Don't you do anything else except sing?" he asked.

"Oh, yes," said the lady. "I look at the moon and I listen to the stars."

"I think it is nicer to play with toys," said Thomas.

"You can play with your horse," said the lady.

Thomas went over to the cockhorse, who was sitting a little way away. The cockhorse was looking at the moon and thinking.

"Well," asked the cockhorse, "how do you like being a toy?"

"I'm not a toy," said Thomas.

"You are one here," said the cockhorse. "Something to talk to, something to sing to, and something to forget when you have got other things to think about."

"I want to go home," said Thomas.

"Well," said the cockhorse, "if you have quite finished the cakes, it's time to go. It's midsummer night again."

"You mean it's midsummer night still," said Thomas.

"No, I don't," said the cockhorse. "Come on, jump on to my back before the lady sees us."

Thomas got on to the cockhorse's back. The cockhorse flicked his tail and jumped straight into the air.

"You are flying," said Thomas.

"I'm not," said the cockhorse. "I'm just thinking."

"And you're not going home. You're going to the moon!"

"Don't you want to go to the moon?" asked the cockhorse.

"Well, perhaps," said Thomas.

The moon got bigger and bluer in the sky. At last it got so big that Thomas was afraid and shut his eyes.

Suddenly the sound of the singing stars stopped. Thomas opened one eye. The stars were still there, but they were colder and smaller. There was a sudden bump.

"Here we are," said the cockhorse.

Beside them was something tall and quiet like a grey tree.

"This isn't the moon," said Thomas. "This is Banbury Cross."

The cockhorse said nothing. He began to trot. Soon Thomas could see a light a long way away.

"That's my home," he said. "And there is my aunt in the window. She is waiting for me."

Thomas jumped off the cockhorse and ran to the door.

"Hello, Aunt," he said. "I'm sorry I'm late, but I was having such a nice time."

"Who is it?" said his aunt. "Who are you?"

"It's me," said Thomas. "It's Thomas."

"Thomas?" said his aunt. "Thomas! I thought you were lost or dead. You ran away a year ago and never came back. Oh, what a bad boy you are! To come home after a year as if you had just been out in the woods to play!"

"But," said Thomas, "but . . . I am only a little late. And I was with a lady."

"Only a little late? A lady?" said his aunt.

"Yes, a fine lady. She had rings on her fingers and bells on her toes and a harp in her hands. She had a great, white horse that could fly through the air and she took me to her house inside a hill to hear the stars singing. She gave me cakes to eat that never make you sick."

"Now don't tell fairy stories," said his aunt.

"I'm not," said Thomas. "I mean I am. I think she was a fairy but I didn't understand everything. But it's true. You ask my cockhorse. He was there too."

The aunt looked at Thomas. Then she looked at the cockhorse lying on the floor. The cockhorse was not looking at her. He was not looking at Thomas. His two glass eyes were pointed straight at the ceiling. His wooden mouth was open. But a cockhorse's mouth is always open.

"Ask your cockhorse?" said his aunt.

"Yes," said Thomas.

The cockhorse said nothing at all.

## 11  A listening library

The second story is more sophisticated than the first in story-line, vocabulary and structure. It comes considerably later in the sequence by which time the learners had gained, if nothing else, facility in following continuous speech. The elements repeated in the story are consequently not so much individual words or structures but whole chunks of language which the learner can virtually reproduce on his own by the end of the story without need of further practice. These chunks contain at least three tenses (the future, simple past, and perfect) employed in natural settings. But, once again, it is not always possible to anticipate what the learner will find most memorable. In this story, all the members of a particular class seized on the word *anywhere,* for example, and used it themselves freely thereafter.

The third story also involves a great deal of repetition and contrast in both vocabulary and structure but in a less obvious way. There is no single teaching point in this story though a learner might learn some things from it. It represents a stage in story-telling (towards the end of their first year with this particular class of beginners) when the learners can listen freely in the language and the story-teller can concentrate on his story-line rather than on his syntax or vocabulary.

These three stories are examples of the kind of listening tape the teacher can use with his class. Eventually he can build up his own listening library containing more varied materials. For beginners we need simple rhymes, stories, jokes and conversations. At a more advanced level we need recordings of poetry, narrative and drama for the learner interested in literature; of talks, lectures and discussions for the learner interested in particular subjects; and of actual conversations in relevant situations for the learner anxious to understand what people may say to him and learn how he should respond. It is not possible to create such a library in a day. But any teacher equipped with a tape-recorder can make a start by recording suitable material from the radio or from gramophone records. He can add a more personal interest to the collection by recording original material scripted by himself or by his pupils. If he can get his pupils to write interesting listening materials of their own design, he will have transformed the laboratory from a centre for extensive listening into an incentive for creative writing.

A library of tapes for use in the laboratory will thus serve four purposes:

1. It will create or sustain in the learner an interest in the language.

2. It will develop his power of understanding and give him a sense of achievement quite independent of his ability to speak.

3. It will give him an opportunity of learning on his own pleasurably, and relatively effortlessly, and we may expect that some of the things he hears will eventually be reproduced in his speech.

4. It will give him a motive, a means and an audience for developing and testing his own powers of putting things into words in the new language.

We cannot expect, of course, that every learner will be able to understand or exploit productively all that he hears in the listening library without further training. Having examined what listening practice may achieve on its own, we shall now turn to a consideration of drills and exercises that are intended to practise systematically the skills of talking and understanding.

NOTES

1. The conversations are so planned, building on what has gone before, that there is in fact seldom any need to consult the translation.
2. These terms were first defined and illustrated in a paper of the same name by D. Abercrombie in *Studies in Phonetics and Linguistics,* Oxford University Press, 1965.
3. There are now available on the market one or two courses that expose the learner to, and give him the chance of studying, unscripted conversation. For example: A. Howatt, J. Webb, M. Knight; *A Modern Course in Business English,* Oxford University Press, 1967; L. Dickinson and R. Mackin: *Varieties of Spoken English,* Oxford University Press, 1969.

# 4    Meaningless drills

*No end to learning,*
*Earn the means first. God surely will contrive*
*Use for our learning.*
       – ROBERT BROWNING: "The Grammarian's Funeral"

## I  The function of drills

Drills are supposed to train the learner to talk by helping him master the basic structural patterns of the language. The object of this chapter and the succeeding one is to enquire how successfully drills achieve this aim. A distinction will be drawn between meaningless and meaningful drills. Both kinds can be used in structural or pronunciation practice. Meaningful drills are, however, less well known, and their possibilities receive a chapter to themselves. "Meaningless" drills are already well-established in the class-room and in the language laboratory. They are usually called "structural drills" or "pattern practice". In this chapter I shall try to show that they may be meaningless in at least two respects. At the same time, I shall assess their effectiveness as a form of structural practice.

Recently a certain amount of dissatisfaction has been voiced against meaningless drills. If such drills fail to give the expected results, it may be because:

1. The drills used are ill-designed or unsuitable in some respect for the learners on whom they are tested.

2. Drills, however well-designed, are an ineffective or limited form of practice.

In the first case we need to discover the principles of designing effective drills. In the second, we must determine the inherent limitations of drills and test them against, or in combination with, alternative forms of practice that might give better results. This chapter will investigate first the scope and then the limitations of traditional types of meaningless drill.

## 2  Types of drill

There are several different ways of classifying drills. The simplest way, which concentrates attention on the scope of drills, is to distinguish between three types:

1. Substitution drills.

2. Mutation drills.[1]

3. Transformation drills.

These terms reflect the nature of the changes the learner has to make in the course of a drill. Every drill starts from a single sentence, an example of a particular structure. The learner's task is to explore the structure by varying the original sentence in a predetermined way. We shall now look at each type of drill in turn.

## 3 Substitution drills

Suppose we want to teach the perfect tense in English, in conjunction with the use of certain adverbs of time. We want the learner to be able to produce utterances such as:

I've already read it.

I've already heard it.

I've already seen it etc.

The simplest way to get him to produce such utterances is to make him repeat them after us. But once he has repeated the first example as a model, there is no need to give him each succeeding example in full. We can prompt him to produce further examples of his own by telling him which verbs we want him to use in each successive sentence. A substitution drill would do this in one of two ways. It could provide the past participle form of each verb in isolation:

| Prompt | Response |
|---|---|
| (i) I've already read it. | *I've already read it.* |
| Heard. | *I've already heard it.* |
| Seen. | *I've already seen it.* |
| Eaten. | *I've already eaten it.* |

or it could embed the past participle in a sentence:

| | |
|---|---|
| (ii) I've already read it. | *I've already read it.* |
| Have you heard it yet? | *I've already heard it.* |
| Have you seen it yet? | *I've already seen it.* |
| Have you eaten it yet? | *I've already eaten it.* |

What the student hears in the course of the drill is printed on the left under the heading *prompt*. What he is expected to say is printed on the right under the heading *response*. In the language laboratory the prompts are generally recorded in advance. A space is left in the tape after each prompt to give the student time to formulate his response. Before being presented with the next prompt, he will hear a correct version of the previous response recorded on the tape. This is supposed to give him the chance of discovering whether he has got each response right. The two drills I have illustrated are very short. An actual drill in the laboratory would probably contain about ten different prompts to give the learner the chance of discovering and exploring the desired pattern of responses. A drill should not be too prolonged, however, or it will risk boring the learner.

The difference between the two types of substitution drill is more apparent than real. Both require the substitution in the previous response of the verb provided in the next prompt. Although the second drill appears to pose the student a series of questions, he does not have to understand the questions or even that he is being asked a question. He merely has to pick out the right word to substitute in the "answers". Notice also that in these, as in all the following drills, the stimulus to which the response is trained is not the prompt by itself. It is the prompt taken in conjunction with the previous response. The prompts merely signal internal changes. What sets the pattern is the series of responses.

## 4 Mutation drills   *Infinitive → past participle*

In the following drills, we will take it for granted that the student has been informed, by repetition or by explicit instruction, which structure he is required to produce. For the moment we will continue to restrict him to sentences in the perfect tense. Instead of giving him ready formed past participles to substitute, as in the two substitution drills, we could provide him with the infinitive form of the verb, either in isolation or as part of a sentence:

*Infinitive*          *Past Participle*

| (i) Read. | *I've already read it.* |
| See. | *I've already seen it.* |
| Hear. | *I've already heard it.* | Changed verbs |
| Eat. | *I've already eaten it.* |

| (ii) Do you want to read it? | *I've already read it.* |
| Do you want to see it? | *I've already seen it.* |
| Do you want to hear it? | *I've already heard it.* |
| Do you want to eat it? | *I've already eaten it.* |

The student no longer has merely to substitute a new verb in each sentence. He must also change its form from infinitive to past participle. Mutation drills, such as these, require systematic changes in the form of words provided in the prompt. They can be used to practise:

1. Word inflection, whether of verbs or nouns. *change = go = went   I do   he does.*

2. Agreement between such constituents of the sentence as subject and verb (or adjective and noun in languages like Spanish and French).

3. Case endings, whether these reveal relationships between nouns and verbs (nominative, accusative, ergative, dative etc.), or are obligatory endings after particular prepositions (genitive, dative, locative, ablative, variously to be found in languages such as Latin, classical Greek, Russian and Bengali).

All the possible types of mutation in English can be illustrated in a single drill:

(iii) Read. [ri:d]          *I've already read it.*
    Eat.                     *I've already eaten it.*
    The boy.              *The boy has already eaten it.*
    More than one boy.    *The boys have already eaten it.*
    More than one thing.  *The boys have already eaten them.*
    Seen you.            *The boys have already seen me.*
    Go.                    *The boys have already been there,*
                         or *gone there.*

This drill is not one for beginners. It is a collapsed form of several possible mutation drills, each practising a separate point. The last example, for instance, involves a contrast between transitive and intransitive verbs, and reveals that the perfect form of a verb may not be lexically or even historically related to its other forms. The choice of the verb *to be* would no longer be optional in the first drill of the next section.

## 5 Transformation drills

Transformation drills may require the substitution of new words in each response, and the mutation of their form. But they also involve a different kind of change:

(i) Do you want to go there? No.    *No, I've already been there.*
    Do you want to hear it? No.    *No, I've already heard it.*
    Do you want to see it? Yes.    *Yes, I haven't seen it yet.*
    Do you want to read it? No.    *No, I've already read it.*
    Do you want to meet him? Yes.  *Yes, I haven't met him yet.*

In this drill the adverb is moved to the end of the sentences in which *not* is inserted. The change of word order is not obligatory. But any drill which requires changes in word order, whether optional or obligatory, which involves the addition or deletion of grammatical constituents such as *not*, and which further exacts the alternation of grammatical pairs like *already* and *yet*, can be called a transformation drill. Transformation drills can accordingly practise:

1. Changes from affirmative to negative.

2. Changes in voice, from active to passive.

3. Changes in mood, from indicative to interrogative to imperative to subjunctive etc.

4. Changes in sentence type from simple to compound or complex.

    All these changes can be worked in either direction. We must be careful, however, to distinguish between drills that genuinely require the learner to transform a sentence, and those that appear to do so, but in fact involve no more than substitution or mutation. The second example of a substitution drill, as has already been noted, and the second example of a mutation drill, like the transformation drill just illustrated, appear to teach the

learner to answer questions. A casual look might make us think that he is
required to change prompt sentences in the interrogative mood into
responses in the indicative. But the learner can get all the responses right
without realising that he is being questioned. The prompt "questions" are
more a camouflage than an essential feature of the drill. They make it look
more natural, but their only relevant function is to provide the learner
with the necessary vocabulary for his responses. We have already seen that
in the case of substitution and mutation drills the vocabulary items can
equally well be supplied in isolation, once the structural pattern of the
response has been indicated. The same is true of the transformation drill
just illustrated, provided we add after each new verb the vital prompt
words *yes* and *no:*

(ii) Go there. No.              *No, I've already been there.*
     Hear it. No.               *No, I've already heard it.*
     See it. Yes.               *Yes, I haven't seen it yet.*

This simplified form of the prompt makes it clearer that the only transformation required in the drill is from positive to negative and back in
succeeding responses.

Transformational changes from simple to compound or complex
sentences are illustrated in the next two drills.

(iii)  You bought the book.      *I have already bought the book*
       You didn't read it.       *but I haven't yet read it.*

       You cooked the food.      *I have already cooked the food*
       You didn't eat it.        *but I haven't yet eaten it.*

       You saw him.              *I have already seen him*
       You didn't meet him.      *but I haven't yet met him.*

(iv)   You bought the record.    *I haven't yet listened to the*
       You didn't listen to it.  *record that I bought.*

       You received a letter.    *I haven't yet answered the*
       You didn't answer it.     *letter that I received.*

       You made some mistakes.   *I haven't yet corrected the*
       You didn't correct them.  *mistakes that I made.*

There is one further use of transformational drills. They can practise the
processes of word derivation.

(v)  He is remarkably honest.       *His honesty is remarkable.*
     He is amazingly intelligent.   *His intelligence is amazing.*
     He is despicably mean.         *His meanness is despicable.*
     It is surprisingly wide.       *Its width is surprising.*
     He is unusually tall.          *His height is unusual.*
     She dances beautifully.        *Her dancing is beautiful.*

As it stands, (v) is a test rather than a drill. Each regular derivational
process it illustrates could be practised in a separate drill. The first four

examples in this one show different ways of forming nouns from adjectives. The fifth example, reminiscent of the relationship between *go* and *be* in previous drills, demonstrates that the noun need not always be lexically related to the adjective. The last example shows that nouns can also be derivationally related to verbs. If the prompts are interchanged with the responses, the drill also practises deriving adverbs of manner from adjectives.

Derivation is a process that can be found in all except the so-called "isolating" languages like Chinese. In German and Bengali it assumes particular importance. For new words can at any time be created according to established derivational rules. To the native speaker such neologisms require neither explanation nor apology. But the foreign learner will be in considerable difficulty unless he knows the rules, for he will not find any of these "words" in the dictionary.

Between them, substitution, mutation and transformation drills can practise all the rules of sentence and word formation in the language.[2] I shall not further illustrate how they do so for English or for other languages. Examples of one or the other type of drill abound in language laboratory manuals such as Stack's, and in all published courses for the laboratory. The examples I have already provided are, moreover, sufficient for us to begin the task of evaluation. But before turning to assessing the value of grammatical drills, I wish to show how the same types of drill may be employed in pronunciation practice.

## 6 Pronunciation drills

System and structure are not the exclusive properties of the grammar of a language. They can also be found in its phonology and in its vocabulary. As far as the phonology is concerned, rules can operate in three areas:

1. The combination of sounds to form syllables or spoken words.

2. The combination of syllables to form rhythmic groupings.

3. The combination of pitch variations to form tone groups, whether these consist of single words as in "tone" languages like Chinese, or of larger units as in "intonation" languages like English.[3]

Unless a learner is confined to pronouncing monosyllabic words, he has to face all three kinds of rule at once. But attention in a drill may be centred on one particular aspect of pronunciation. In the following substitution drill the learner is apparently producing a series of sentences of the same structural type in which the rhythm and intonation are held constant. What varies is the vowel or the final consonant in a single word. The object of the drill is to give practice in vowel and consonant contrasts.

| (i) A bead maker. | *A bead maker makes beads.* |
| A bidder. | *A bidder makes bids.* |
| A bed maker. | *A bed maker makes beds.* |

| A better. | *A better makes bets.* |
|-----------|------------------------|
| A bat maker. | *A bat maker makes bats.* |
| A butt maker. | *A butt maker makes butts.* |
| A boot maker. | *A boot maker makes boots.* |
| A boat maker. | *A boat maker makes boats.* |

One or two of the responses illustrate a limitation of this kind of drill. Some learners might not know, for instance, that a "butt" was something to shoot at. They could still complete the drill successfully. Such pronunciation drills may be, or may become, quite empty of sense as far as the learner is concerned.

The second example is also a substitution drill. But its purpose is different. Its aim is to give practice in preserving a stress pattern despite an increase in the number of syllables in the rhythmic group.

| (ii) Poll's doll was sick, sick, sick. | *Poll's doll was sick, sick, sick.* |
|-----------------------------------------|--------------------------------------|
| Miss. | *Miss Poll's doll was sick, sick, sick.* |
| Polly's. | *Miss Polly's doll was sick, sick, sick.* |
| Dolly. | *Miss Polly's dolly was sick, sick, sick.* |
| Had a dolly who. | *Miss Polly had a dolly who was sick, sick, sick.* |
| A little dolly. | *Miss Polly had a little dolly who was sick, sick, sick.* |
| Very sick. | *Miss Polly had a little dolly who was very sick, sick, sick.* |

Each successive prompt inserts extra syllables into the response without, however, changing the number of stresses in the line. Each response should be spoken with only four stresses occurring at roughly regular intervals of time. The stresses fall on the syllables *Poll* and *doll,* and on the first and third occurrences of the word *sick.* Such a drill would have very different results in syllable-timed languages such as French, Spanish and Bengali, where each syllable rather than each foot takes about the same amount of time to say. Here the length of the sentence (in terms of time), and the number of stresses, would increase in direct proportion to the number of syllables. In these languages, we would have to call it a transformational drill, since it would add more rhythmic elements to the sentence.            *The shifting of stress*

The next two drills test the placing of stress in derivationally related nouns and verbs. The stress is shifted from one syllable to another according to whether the "word" is functioning as a noun or a verb. This phenomenon of variable word stress is technically called *accent:*

| (iii) Rebels | *Rebels rebel.* |
|--------------|-----------------|
| Permits. | *Permits permit.* |
| Torments. | *Torments torment.* |
| Insults. | *Insults insult.* |
| Portraits. | *Portraits portray.* |
| Photographers. | *Photographers photograph.* |

(iv) Dancers.            *Dancers dance dances.*
     Importers.          *Importers import imports.*
     Exporters.          *Exporters export exports.*
     Composers.       *Composers compose compositions.*
     Subjectors.        *Subjectors subject subjects.*

The next example, practising changes in intonation, is clearly transformational:

(v) A birt in the hand.       *A birt in the hand?*
    To drive the guill.       *To drive the guill?*
    To live from hand to month.    *To live from hand to month?*
    Empty vessels sound much.    *Empty vessels sound much?*
    Like dog, like hammer.     *Like dog, like hammer?*
    We were increasing this
    second edition with a
    phraseology and with        *With a phraseology and with*
    idiotisms.             *idiotisms?*

The examples are drawn from a list of useful English proverbs in a Bengali Dictionary and from a Portuguese Guide to English Conversation[4]. The drill provokes *echo questions,* the transformation of statements into questions by a shift in intonation. For this purpose it is not unreasonable to present the learner with examples of odd or faulty English. In real life he may often hear things said whose sense at first escapes him. The echo question is a technique of eliciting clarification or confirmation.

Intonation practice is not confined to transformation drills. All drills, whether grammatical or phonological, which preserve a constant pitch pattern in the responses are substitution drills from the point of view of intonation. For that matter all grammatical drills give practice in sound combinations and rhythmic groupings as well as intonation. The question we must now investigate is how far they practise anything else.

## 7   The limitations of drills

We have seen how structural drills are supposed to train the learner to talk through repeating and varying a series of structural patterns. To succeed in this aim, two separate steps must be completed. The learner must correctly apprehend the nature of the different structures drilled. He must also learn to use them when they are needed. But drills may fail to help him in either respect. In their very nature they suffer from four limitations. These relate to:

1. The tum-te-tum effect.

2. The absence of meaning.

3. The nature of the stimulus.

4. The risk of over-generalisation.

# 8  The tum-te-tum effect

In this chapter I have described drills as practising the production of structures. This is certainly their intention. But the intentions may run foul of the principle of least effort. A learner may not learn unless he has to. And traditional drills can often be successfully performed without any attention being paid to the structure. This is a consequence of the tum-te-tum effect. It occurs in its purest form in substitution drills. Since the structure does not change throughout the drill, it may not be heard at all. It becomes simply a background noise, which can be replaced without loss by the sounds *tum* and *te*. The effect can be illustrated with drill (i) of section 4, a drill supposedly practising the perfect tense.

Suppose the syllable *tum* stands for every stressed syllable, and the syllable *te* for every unstressed one. Further, suppose the words *tonk, konk, bonk* etc. stand for every new vocabulary item. The drill will now go:

| | |
|---|---|
| Tum tumtete tonk te. | *Tum tumtete tonk te.* |
| Konk. | *Tum tumtete konk te.* |
| Bonk. | *Tum tumtete bonk te.* |
| Honk. | *Tum tumtete honk te.* |

The effect may seem a little far-fetched. But a learner can in fact go through a drill without having the slightest idea of what he is practising. This may be brought home if the reader attempts for himself the next example of a Bengali structural drill.[5] It is better to cover the right hand side of the page with a sheet of paper, moving it down the page as each new prompt is tackled.

| | |
|---|---|
| Ami ekhoni eṭa dekhechi. | *ami ekhoni eṭa dekhechi.* |
| shun- | *ami ekhoni eṭa shunechi.* |
| por- | *ami ekhoni eṭa porechi.* |
| kin- | *ami ekhoni eṭa kinechi.* |
| khe- | *ami ekhoni eṭa kheechi.* |

At first it may be difficult to identify the syllable to be substituted in each successive response. But by the end of the drill this has established itself and the reader could probably produce further prompted examples of the same pattern with little effort. The unwary teacher, hearing you hard at work in the laboratory, might think that you were intentionally producing examples of the perfect tense in Bengali. For the original sentence meant:

I just now it seen have. (I have just seen it.)

And verb stems meaning *hear, read, buy* and *eat* were successively substituted. But from your point of view, you might just as well have been reproducing *tums* and *te's*. The only changes allowed in the drill were changes of vocabulary items, or the combination of sounds that represent them. Even these changes were controlled by the prompts. There was no

*substitution drills*
*+ contrastive drills*

element of choice. And it appears that when there is no choice, when a structural pattern is invariant, the structure itself fades into the background. Structure of necessity implies choice. When choice is not permitted, as in substitution drills, there is a risk that all that is being practised is pronunciation.

Contrastive drills, as their name suggests, exact a structural choice. From this point of view, both drill (ii) (mutation) and drill (i) (transformation) are contrastive drills. The first permits the student to choose the wrong inflectional form for irregular verbs — "heared" instead of "heard" — and the second requires a choice between affirmative and negative forms of a sentence. But it does not follow that contrastive drills necessarily teach the correct formation of structures. The stories of Shanace and Jeeto in Chapter 2 revealed that the learner may mistake the kind of choice that is involved. Grammatical restrictions may be "understook"[6] as free stylistic variations. The learner may make all the correct choices in the drill without realising that any other form of response would have been incorrect. He has learnt what is right, but the absence of explanations may result in his failing to discover what is wrong.

## 9   The absence of meaning

Two further limitations of drills have been illustrated in earlier chapters. The Bengali drill, as far as the reader was concerned, was entirely meaningless. So, in a slightly different sense, is any drill that permits no choice of vocabulary. If he cannot choose his own words, the learner has no control over the meaning of what he says in a drill. His responses convey no information to anyone apart from himself. And, in the effort to produce particular sounds or structures correctly, the student himself may pay no attention to the meaning of what he is saying. Or so a teacher was told by her class of fifteen year old girls learning French in the language laboratory of an Edinburgh school. Many of them commented that "you don't have to understand", "after a little you don't remember even to try to understand what you are doing", "it just becomes parroting."

## 10   The nature of the stimulus

In behaviourist terms, the object of a drill is to train a response to a stimulus. The behaviourist may achieve his object only too well. All too often a student who can correctly produce a structure in the drill situation will not use it in any other. I have watched a group of students work happily through a most carefully planned set of substitution and contrastive drills on the perfect tense. Shortly after emerging from the language laboratory, they were asked if they had seen a particular film.

These were some of their replies:

Yes.

Yes, I have seen.

I have already seen.

I already saw it.

I have already enjoyed.

In actual communication, the students made all the mistakes, grammatical and lexical, that the drills were supposed to forestall. Even if some kind of structural learning takes place, it must be conceded that drills provide a setting — both in the ordinary sense of the word and in the psychologist's — for only one kind of speech, which I have previously referred to as "structurespeech". They do not practise when to use a particular structure, or when not to, in relation to a wider situation. Accordingly, they give no indication of what the structure means.

## 11  The risk of over-generalisation

Most students will not long tolerate the situation I placed you in with the Bengali drill. If they hear a new word in a drill, they will want to know what it means. And of course, they will want to know what the structure means and what the rules for its formation are. Since the drill itself does not tell them, they must rely on what they have understood from our initial presentation, and whatever they may further gain by rapidly translating the examples into their mother tongue. In the case of the English perfect tense, this may prove a disastrous procedure.

Suppose a keen student applies his mind as well as his ears to the job, and sets about consciously learning to produce a structure. For the perfect tense, this would mean learning to preserve a certain word order, inflecting the verbs, and performing any indicated transformations in sentence type. What sort of things may he say when he comes out of the laboratory? The following utterances are genuine instances of students' attempts to apply drilled structures in real life:

Already Mary had bought the car.

I have already liked it.

I have ever lived in Calcutta.     *Have you ever?*

The first sentence is possible but it is an inappropriate response to the question that elicited it: 'Has she bought it yet?' The remaining two examples display mistakes in the application of mutation and transformation rules. It so happens that certain verbs in English — *like, know, believe* — can occur only in restricted contexts in the perfect (and also in the continuous) tense forms. When they do so occur, they are often used emphatically or in a sense different from that which they normally possess. The word *ever*, in the third example, is one of those words in English — like *much* and *any* when they are used as quantifiers — which usually only occur in questions and negative sentences.

All three mistakes, and many others could be cited of different structures, are mistakes of over-generalisation. Where the drills were supposed to suggest restrictions of word order and word occurrence, the learner has seen only invitations to experiment. There is nothing bad about this. We want the student to produce utterances that he has never heard before. And, we may want him to make this kind of mistake if only to learn why he should not do so again. But drills, whether contrastive or not, have set themselves an impossible task implemented by an impossible technique. They attempt to forestall all mistakes while at the same time showing only positive instances of what can be done. Negative instances are not given in drills, so the learner cannot find out where or when the rule does not apply.

## 12 An ambiguity

The phrase "to produce an utterance" conceals a quadruple ambiguity. It may mean:

1. To produce a set of noises that are intelligible to a native hearer but have neither sense nor grammatical structure for the speaker.

2. To produce an example of a grammatical structure consciously, without intending to convey any information to any hearer, and without fully knowing the rules that govern its formation or application.

3. To produce an utterance correctly, in full knowledge of the rules, intending to convey information to a hearer.

4. To produce an utterance incorrectly, from the point of view of grammar or style, which may nonetheless convey the desired information to the hearer.

If we consider these four possibilities as objectives, the first and the second are the only two aimed at by traditional drills.[7] They are both achieved in the language laboratory. The consequence outside it is the fourth possibility. In so far as the third possibility is achieved by the way, we can say that drills are a preparation for talking. They are not a training for it — they train responses to a totally irrelevant kind of stimulus — and they may not be a necessary preparation.

## 13 A paradox

This review of the limitations of traditional drills — the tum-te-tum effect, their meaninglessness, the artificiality of the stimulus, the risk of over-generalisation — has led to a paradox. I have offered two contradictory answers to the question of whether drills do or do not practise structures. On the one hand, I have argued that they may fail to do so, at least in the case of substitution drills, and at least to the extent of neglecting to distinguish syntactic from stylistic criteria in the case of contrastive drills. On the other hand, I have argued that they teach structures all too successfully. By declining to give negative examples, they encourage the student to make mistakes of over-generalisation.

It seems to me that both results are possible, though neither is intended. This is because the results depend more on what the learner actually reads into a drill than on what its designer imagines it is practising. A slow or tired student may fail to absorb the structural point. I have shown that it is possible to do so and still complete the drill with all apparent signs of success. Alternatively, a keen student may jump to conclusions about the nature of the structure which the drill was never meant to suggest. In either case, the character or extent of learning that the drill actually promotes cannot be assessed inside the laboratory. The real test comes outside when the student is called upon to use the structure in appropriate contexts.

Even if a learner appears to be learning a lot from drills, this does not prove that it is the drills that are doing the work. The pupils may be learning *despite,* not because of, the drills. There is again only one test. Other techniques of practice must be tried to see if they achieve equally good or better results. Exercises and problems are available as additional or alternative materials, and there is no reason why drills should continue to be meaningless, as I shall show in the next chapter.

NOTES

1. I have borrowed this term from E. M. Stack: *The Language Laboratory in Modern Language Teaching,* Oxford University Press, 1960.
2. Linguists such as Chomsky customarily distinguish between three types of rule (phrase-structure, selectional and transformational) in terms of which all the sentences in a language can be described. See *Aspects of the Theory of Syntax,* Massachusetts Institute of Technology Press, 1964. Each type of drill can be directly related to a corresponding type of rule, in the sense that substitution drills practise the application of phrase-structure rules etc.
3. For a full discussion of these terms, and of the various domains of phonetics and phonology, see D. Abercrombie: *Elements of General Phonetics,* Edinburgh University Press, 1967.
4. Professor Pedro Carolino, *New Guide of the Conversation,* 1869, reprinted under the title of *English as she is Wrotten,* Scouse Press, Liverpool, 1967.
5. The phonetic transcription is my own. For the purpose of the example, it does not matter how the symbols are pronounced.
6. This term, a blend of "understand" and "mistook", is drawn from Professor Carolino's *New Guide,* op. cit.
7. See Chapter 2.

# 5 Meaningful drills

*Language without meaning is like a chicken
without its head.*

— ROMAN JAKOBSON

## I  Application drills

Suppose we were to put a picture as a prompt in the left hand column:

(i)

Felicity is eating a fish.

Felicity has just eaten the fish.

Felicity is climbing a mountain.

Felicity has just climbed the mountain.

Felicity is combing her hair.

Felicity has just combed her hair.

Felicity is going into a cinema.

Felicity has just come out of the cinema.

*[handwritten note:]* sequenceg pictures = seay lenses PG 64

If we look down the right hand column, we can see that the student is still doing a structural drill. The drill requires the substitution of new verbs and nouns, and it contrasts two tense forms, the continuous and the perfect. Some of the responses also contrast the articles *a* and *the*. This is only necessary if each pair of pictures is taken as showing a sequence of events. If the pictures contrasted the activities of Felicity with those of someone else, we could use the indefinite article throughout.

But what has happened to the prompt? It no longer verbally supplies the words that are to be substituted. Furthermore, the contrast between tenses is no longer verbally cued. It, too, is suggested by the differences in content of the pictures, just as the contrastive use of articles is controlled by the similarities. The relationship between prompt and response, between each picture and the utterance that describes it, is a meaningful relationship. It is often called a relationship of "reference", but I shall follow Lyons[1] in using the wider term "application". We can define application relationships as those holding between sentences in the language and situations or states of affairs in the world.

The relationship between successive prompts and responses is a meaningful relationship, and we can therefore call the drill itself a meaningful drill. The relationship between successive responses, however, is structural. Meaningful drills, just like meaningless ones, depend on the techniques of substitution, mutation and transformation discussed in the previous chapter. They can thus equally be used to practise all the grammatical rules of the language. But they may also be subject to some of the limitations of meaningless drills. The successful completion of a drill, moreover, depends on the student already possessing an adequate knowledge of meaning relationships in the language. But, in places, his knowledge may be defective, or it may lead him to offer an alternative interpretation to the one expected by the teacher. In response to the final prompt of the previous drill, for instance, the student might say: *Felicity has just been to the cinema.*

Pictures are necessarily ambiguous. What we can do about the student's alternative "readings" will be discussed a little later. For the moment let us profit from this ambiguity by using pictures to elicit quite different kinds of structures. The reader can test how effectively they do so by keeping the responses covered while he looks at the prompts.

(ii)

This is mother.

This is father.

This is Felicity.

   This is Anthony.

This is a cat.

This is the sun.

This is a bird.

(iii)

1. Mother is in the kitchen.

2. Father is in the sitting room.

3. Felicity is in a bedroom.

4. Anthony is in the bathroom.

5. The cat is in a tree.

6. The trees are in the garden.

7. The bird is on the roof.

8. The sun is in the sky.[2]

Finally, by using close-ups of the numbered scenes of the previous picture:

(iv)

   Mother is lighting the stove.

Father is watching television.

Felicity is sleeping.

Anthony is having a bath.

The cat is watching the bird.

The bird is singing.

The sun is shining.

Drill (ii) practises naming people and things, an operation which requires the omission of articles before all the proper nouns. Drill (iii) practises the use of prepositions; the use of the definite article before "unique" nouns like *bathroom* and *garden* or before the already mentioned noun *cat*; and the use of the indefinite article where there is more than one object to which the noun might refer. There are two bedrooms and two trees in the picture. Drill (iv) uses the same pictures to elicit different verbs, both transitive and intransitive, and continues to practise the use and omission of articles.

Notice that in drill (i), the sequence of pictures established a sequence of tenses. In these latter drills, the pictures are all simultaneous, though obviously they have to be presented and responded to in a certain order. The natural tense to use in such a case is the present tense for naming and for locating individuals, and the present continuous for describing their activities.

Let us look at one more set of pictures:

You can't drive faster than thirty miles an hour here.

You must stop here.

You can't turn right here.

You can't go down there.

You must drive slowly here.

You can't overtake here.

You must drive carefully here.

You can't park here.

Strictly speaking, the prompts in this drill are signs, not pictures. They are signs which both require and elicit explanations. In these examples the explanations involve a transformational contrast between positive and negative sentences, in which *can't* is the appropriate negative counterpart to *must*. A different sense of *can't* is illustrated in the last example. If the verb were to be used consistently, the sign should read:

         NO PARKING

Equivalent signs in French could contrast the uses of *devoir* and *pouvoir,* in Spanish of *deber* and *poder,* in Bengali of *hobe na* and *parbe na,* in Latin of *licet* and *posse.*

Picture prompts can thus be used to practise the production of isolated utterances (substitution), the contrast between related sentences (mutation and transformation), and the building up of connected narrative or description. Successful achievement of any of these aims depends on a knowledge of relevant application relationships. The use of signs presupposes, in addition, a certain knowledge of the world. For the interpretation of verbal signs requires more than an understanding of what the words refer to. You must also know what the whole sign implies — i.e. you must know the Highway Code.

We shall now look at drills which call upon the student's knowledge of the world without the aid of picture prompts.

## 2  General knowledge drills

(i) Rod Laver.                *Rod Laver plays tennis.*
    Paul McCartney.          *Paul McCartney plays the guitar.*
    Yehudi Menuhin.         *Yehudi Menuhin plays the violin.*
    Pelé.                    *Pelé plays football.*

| Arnold Palmer. | *Arnold Palmer plays golf.* |
| Gary Sobers. | *Gary Sobers plays cricket.* |
| Pablo Casals. | *Pablo Casals plays the cello.*[3] |
| You yourself? | |

This drill also practises the use of articles in English but in a different
setting. The student has to learn when to use, and when not to use, the
definite article after a verb like *play*. In French, the same drill would
present a choice between the prepositions *à* and *de*. While in Spanish and
in Bengali, it would become a vocabulary drill, testing the use of the verbs
*tocar* and *jugar*, *baja* and *khela* respectively.

The last example in the drill is a "joker". It breaks the pattern of
response, quite deliberately, to make the student think. If only as a means
of reducing the tum-te-tum effect, such anomalous prompts have their
own value, though it is not possible to anticipate how the student will
answer them. We cannot, therefore, "reward" this kind of response by
acquainting the student with the right answer on the tape.

| (ii) The Queen. ( *her own pl* ) | *The Queen lives in Buckingham Palace.* |
| The President of the | *The President lives in the White House.* |
| United States. *Public Hse* | |
| The British Prime Minister. | *The British Prime Minister lives at 10,* |
| | *Downing Street.* |
| The Pope. | *The Pope lives in the Vatican.* |
| Sherlock Holmes. | *Sherlock Holmes lived at 221B, Baker* |
| | *Street.* |
| The Three Bears. | *The Three Bears lived in a house in a* |
| ( *Common noun* ) | *wood.* |
| You yourself? | |

This drill practises the use of prepositions and articles before different
kinds of place names, and a meaningful contrast between present and past
tenses. It also illustrates that we can call upon the student's knowledge of
the world of fiction as well as that of fact.

## 3  Sound effect drills

The language laboratory is an obvious place for aural sound effects. They
can be used as background noise to contextualise a conversation, or as
prompts in a drill.

| (i) (Wuf, wuf.) | *I can hear a dog barking.* |
| (Tweet, tweet.) | *I can hear a bird singing.* |
| (Drip, drip.) | *I can hear a tap dripping.* |
| (Wa, wa.) | *I can hear a baby crying.* |
| (Clap, clap.) | *I can hear some people clapping.* |
| (pffff.) | *I can hear someone breathing.* |
| (Ha! Ha!) | *I can hear someone laughing.* |
| (Silence.) | *I can't hear anything now.* |

This drill practises the use of a participle after a verb — it would require an infinitive and a change of word order in French — the use of the articles *a* and *some,* and the use of positive and negative forms of indefinite pronouns.

Sound effects could also be used in a slightly different way, not as the focus of attention and commentary, but as vocabulary cues:

(ii) How did Felicity go home?
     (Vroom, vroom.)           *She went by car.*
     And Anthony? (Hoot, hoot.)    *He went by ship.*
     And mother? (Chuff, chuff.)    *She went by train.*
     And father? (Ting-a-ling.)     *He went by bicycle.*
     And the cat? (Pitter, patter.)    *It went on foot.*
     And the bird? (Whush, whush.)  *It flew.*

This drill contrasts the use of the prepositions *by* and *on* in English, *à* and *en* in French. In Russian and in German it would contrast the use of different verbs. The same responses could, incidentally, be prompted by pictures. In general, the possibilities of sound effects are more limited than those of pictures, because fewer sounds can be identified with certainty. It would be difficult, for example, to distinguish aurally, but not visually, a bus from a car or a lorry. On the other hand, it would be difficult to convey pictorially, but not aurally, the sense of sentences such as: *she sighed, he talks too fast,* or *it's hollow.*

The final prompt and response in the drill introduce a different kind of meaning relationship which we shall call collocation.

## 4  Collocation drills

(i) This is a wonderful book.      *Good, I'd like to read it.*
    This is a fantastic record.     *Good, I'd like to hear it.*
    Mr. Lock is a very amusing
    speaker.                    *Good, I'd like to hear him.*
    Felicity is a very nice girl.    *Good, I'd like to meet her.*
    There's an interesting
    programme on T.V. tonight.   *Good, I'd like to watch it.*
    There's a good film at the
    cinema this week.           *Good, I'd like to see it.*
    It's called "Gunfight at
    the O.K. Corral".          *Good, I like cowboy films.*

The structural point is plain. It is the contrast between *would like to* and *like.* What is not quite so obvious is the nature of the meaning relationship between prompt and response. It is exclusively a verbal relationship because neither pictures nor sound effects are involved. Only the last response requires any knowledge of the world. The remainder depend on a knowledge of lexical inter-dependencies. The student must know that books are things you read, rather than meet or hear.

Although there is considerable freedom in the language about who may be said to do what with what to whom, there are also certain restrictions. These are taken for granted by the native speaker who may only become aware of them when they are broken. We can all, for example, see that something odd is said in this apocryphal incident from *Alice through the Looking Glass:*

The White Queen unceremoniously placed her head in Alice's lap and fell asleep. Alice herself dozed off but was woken by the gentle snoring of the queen. Her legs began to ache. She moved them cautiously, disturbing the queen who sat up with a start. "Goodness, you slept a long time," said Alice, trying to excuse herself. "No, I didn't," said the queen offended. "It's just that I sleep more slowly than you do."

We talk about running slowly or for a long time, so why can't we also sleep slowly? Queens do not do impossible things even in Wonderland. They merely exercise their prerogative to break conventions. In this case, we are concerned with verbal conventions, with rules and restrictions governing the lexical combination of words. Like other rules they have to be learnt, and they may cause the learner unexpected difficulties if he thinks of the conventions of his own language as universally applicable. But in so far as the collocational rules in the new language have been mastered, we can call upon them to obtain appropriate responses in drills.

Collocational relationships are not bound to a particular type of structure, any more than pictures are. The same kind of link between verb and object that was employed in the previous drill prompts a quite different structure in the next one:

(ii)  Read these sentences aloud, filling in the blanks.

1.  Do you like going abroad? I used to travel ...........................................
    but I haven't travelled much recently.
    *I used to travel a lot but I haven't travelled much recently.*

2.  Do you like fruit? I used to ..................................... but I haven't
    ...........................recently.
    *I used to eat a lot but I haven't eaten much recently.*

3.  Do you like tennis? I used to ................................................................
    but I...................................................................................... recently.
    *I used to play a lot but I haven't played much recently.*

4.  Do you like poetry? I .........................................................................
    but.......................................................................................................
    *I used to read a lot but I haven't read much recently.*

5.  Do you like tobacco? I.........................................................................
    ............................................................................................................
    *I used to smoke a lot but I haven't smoked much recently.*

> { abroad
> { fruit
> { tennis
> Travel – abroad?
> eat – fruit
> plas – tennis

The structural point in this drill is the contrast between *much* and *a lot*, *much* being restricted to the negative clause in each sentence. The collocational relationship between the nouns in the prompts and the verbs in the responses is only incidental to this structural contrast and to the alternation of tenses. But it forces the student to think out each sentence. The drill is presented in a programmed format. This will be familiar from the Novish lesson. The student follows written prompts, but speaks his answers into the tape-recorder, on which a model version has been recorded. A programmed format is convenient whenever we want the student to vary something in the middle of a sentence, and when the sentence itself is long. The student starts by reading aloud the greater part of the sentence, but as the drill progresses, the prompt slowly vanishes — like the Cheshire cat or the words of "John Brown's Body" — leaving only the blank behind.

The collocational relationship exploited in the previous two drills was held between a verb and its object. There are also conventions relating a subject to the verb. In the next example these are used to elicit examples of the perfect tense.

(iii) Is William a playwright, then?  *Yes, he's just written a new play.*
　　 Is Jane a novelist, then?  *Yes, she's just written a new novel.*
　　 Is Pablo a painter, then?  *Yes, he's just painted a new picture.*
　　 Is Igor a composer, then?  *Yes, he's just composed a new piece of music.*
　　 Is Frank an architect, then?  *Yes, he's just designed a new building.*
　　 Is Laurence an actor, then?  *Yes, he's just acted in a new play.*

The same prompts could also elicit statements in the simple present tense (*Yes, he writes plays etc.*). If we turn our attention to the relationship between the producer and the product implicit in the last drill we can embark on a new structure:

(iv) I like that picture  *Do you know who the artist is?*
　　 I like that building.  *Do you know who the architect is?*
　　 I like this piece of music.  *Do you know who the composer is?*
　　 I like this sculpture.  *Do you know who the sculptor is?*
　　 I like this book.  *Do you know who the author is?* — who is he?

The student is, of course, engaged in asking indirect questions, a notorious source of difficulty for all foreign learners of English.

A further form of collocation relationship involves what film directors call "the location". Films are made in studios and shown in cinemas. Beer is made in vats and drunk in pubs. The next drill is concerned with establishing the whereabouts of some important places. The speaker in the drill is a tourist.

(v) You want to change some  *Can you tell me where the nearest money.*  *bank is?*

You want to buy some stamps.    *Can you tell me where the nearest post office is?*

You want to buy some cigarettes.    *Can you tell me where the nearest tobacconist's is?*

You want to buy a newspaper.    *Can you tell me where the nearest newsagent's is?*

You want to find a taxi.    *Can you tell me where the nearest taxi stand is?*

After all that shopping,
you need a drink.

Finally, collocation relationships may hold between adjectives and verbs.

(vi)

1. I tried to do the sum. But the sum was so difficult that I couldn't ........
............
   *The sum was so difficult that I couldn't do it.*

2. I tried to lift the box. But the box was so .................. that I couldn't
...................... .
   *The box was so heavy that I couldn't lift it.*

3. There was too much chilli in my curry. The curry was ..........................
...........that I couldn't ........................
   *The curry was so hot that I couldn't eat it.*

4. Felicity gave her mother a cup of coffee. The coffee ......................
........... that she couldn't...........................
   *The coffee was so hot that she couldn't drink it.*

5. I got a letter from a friend yesterday. But his handwriting..................
.................................................................................................. .
   *His handwriting was so illegible,* or *poor,* or *bad, that I couldn't read it.*

6. My teacher asked me a question. But ..................................................
.................................................................................................. .
   *The question was so difficult that I couldn't answer it.*

This drill practises the use of *so* before an adjective. It could obviously lead on to further drills in which the final pronoun was varied, and to contrastive drills with *such......that* and *too,* in the latter case the final pronoun being omitted. A similar problem arises in French with *si grand que* and *trop grand pour.*

## 5  Implication relationships

In the fifth response of the last drill, the adjectives *poor, bad* and *illegible* were all offered as alternative descriptions of the friend's handwriting. In this context, though in few others, they are synonymous — that is, they have the same meaning and can be interchanged. Synonymy is not a type of application or collocation relationship. It is an example of a new kind of meaning relationship called implication.

1. **Application** is the name we gave to the relationship between words and things, between sentences in the language and events or states of affairs in the world. When we ask what a sentence or a word means we are interested in its application.

2. **Collocation** is the name we gave to the relationship between different classes of words in the language. It is concerned with which adjectives are commonly associated with which nouns, or which nouns with which verbs etc. Thus in the last drill the adjective *hot* was applied to the nouns *curry* and *coffee,* though referring to a different quality in each case.

3. **Implication** is the name we shall give to relationships holding between words occurring in different sentences. When we ask whether two words, such as *poor* and *bad,* mean the same thing, or are opposites, we are concerned with implications. Synonymy and antonymy are two kinds of implication relationship. There are three further kinds whose functioning we shall also study in drills.

## 6  Synonymy drills

Usually we think of synonymy as applying to words of the same class. Thus we may enquire whether two adjectives are synonymous, or two verbs, or two nouns. But in many cases, synonymy relates different classes of word or phrase. In the following example simple verbs in the prompt are expanded to more complex predicates in the response. The grammatical point is the use of certain prepositions with verbs of motion.

(i) Father walked here.      *He came on foot.*
Mother flew here.      *She came by plane.*
Felicity drove here.    *She came by car.*
Oedipus cycled here.   *He came by bicycle.*
Columbus sailed there.  *He went by ship.*
The three messengers rode
from Ghent to Aix.    *They went on horseback.*

Alternatively, a whole predicate can be replaced by an adjective. In the following drill, the adjective is preceded by *very.*

(ii) Father earns a lot of money.  *He's very rich.*
Anthony makes a lot of noise.  *He's very noisy.*
Felicity makes little noise.  *She's very quiet.*
Mother doesn't have much
spare time.    *She's very busy.*
She doesn't get enough sleep.  *She's very tired.*
I don't do any work.    *You're very lazy.*

An adjective can be replaced by a quantifier to practise the contrast between *much* and *a lot.*

(iii) The teapot is almost empty.       *There's not much tea left.*
      The coffee tin is almost full.    *There's a lot of coffee left.*
      The sugar bowl is almost
      empty.                            *There's not much sugar left.*
      The river bed is almost dry.      *There's not much water left.*
      The ultimatum has almost
      expired.                          *There's not much time left.*
      That page is almost empty.        *There's a lot of space left.*
      My bank account is almost
      empty.                            *There's not much money left.*
      The chocolate box is almost
      empty.                            *There are not many chocolates left.*

An adjective clause can also be replaced by a modal verb. The next drill practises the grammatical contrast between *mustn't* and *needn't.*

(iv) *The Reading Lesson: Notes to Teachers*

1. It is essential that you don't spend too long on explanations.
   *I mustn't spend too long on explanations.*

2. It is not essential to translate every word.
   *I needn't translate every word.*

3. It is not necessary that the pupils understand every word during your first reading.
   *The pupils needn't understand every word during my first reading.*

4. But it is essential that they don't read entirely mechanically.
   *They mustn't read entirely mechanically.*

5. If labels and charts are used to develop word and sentence recognition, it is essential that they are not left in the same place day after day.
   *Labels and charts mustn't be left in the same place day after day.*

6. It is not necessary for the pupils to read the passage aloud.
   *The pupils needn't read the passage aloud.*

7. If they do do so, there is no need for you to let only one pupil read aloud at a time.
   *I needn't let only one pupil read aloud at a time.*[4]

8. But it is necessary that you check each pupil's reading from time to time.
   *I must check each pupil's reading from time to time.*

In the next example, a noun phrase is replaced by a synonymous noun phrase. The object is to contrast the prepositions *since* and *for,* and to practise intonation patterns that express irony.

(v) I've been waiting for 15 minutes.
*Have you really been waiting for quarter of an hour?*

Felicity's been waiting for 30 minutes.
*Has she really been waiting for half an hour?*

Anthony has been ready for the last 45 minutes.
*Has he really been ready for three quarters of an hour?*

Father's been waiting since 25th December.
*Has he really been waiting since Christmas?*

Mother waited for seven days.
*Did she really wait for a week?*

Finally, a noun phrase can be expanded into a whole clause — a relative clause in the next example:

| | |
|---|---|
| (vi) A tobacconist. | *A tobacconist is a man who sells cigarettes and tobacco.* |
| A greengrocer. | *A greengrocer is a man who sells fruit and vegetables.* |
| A butcher. | *A butcher is a man who sells meat.* |
| A baker. | *A baker is a man who sells bread and cakes.* |
| A candlestick maker. | *A candlestick maker is a man who makes candlesticks.* |
| A sculptor. | *A sculptor is a man who makes statues.* |
| An architect. | *An architect is a man who designs buildings.* |
| A chauffeur. | *A chauffeur is a man who drives cars.* |
| A screwdriver. | *A screwdriver is a tool which drives in screws.* |
| A hammer. | *A hammer is a tool which drives in nails.* |
| A record-player | *A record-player is a machine that plays records.* |
| A camera. | *A camera is a machine that takes photographs.* |
| A loudspeaker. | *A loudspeaker is a machine that amplifies sound.* |
| A barometer. | *A barometer is an instrument which measures pressure.* |
| A thermometer. | *A thermometer is an instrument which measures temperature.* |
| A swimming pool. | *A swimming pool is a place where you can swim.* |

A library.                              *A library is a place where you can*
                                        *borrow books.*

A hotel.                                *A hotel is a place where you can stay.*

This drill could, and probably should, be broken into a number of separate drills, each dealing with a different kind of relative clause, and each type of clause raising further contrasts glimpsed in earlier drills i.e. countable and uncountable nouns; transitive and intransitive verbs. As it stands, it tests all these grammatical points by appeal to general knowledge, and to collocation as well as to synonymy relationships. Throughout the drill there is also an implicit use of a new kind of implication relationship: *hyponymy.* Hyponymy is a relationship of inclusion. Thus the screwdriver and hammer mentioned in the drill are both tools, while the barometer and thermometer belong to the class of instruments. In these examples the hyponymous relationship holds between nouns. In the next section we shall see that it can relate other parts of speech.

## 7  Hyponymy drills

*children*

The first example shows one more approach to the problems of countable and uncountable nouns. The student has to choose an inclusive term for the various nouns mentioned in the prompts, and to quantify it with an appropriate determiner.

(i)

1. The old woman who lived in a shoe had a lot of sons and daughters.
   There   were .................................that she couldn't feed them all.
   *There were so many children that she couldn't feed them all.*

2. There were a lot of dahlias, roses and marigolds in the garden.
   There ........................................ that I couldn't pick ................... all.
   *There were so many flowers that I couldn't pick them all.*

3. For dinner, she gave me a huge amount of rice and chicken.
   There ............................................that   I   couldn't ..........
   ............ all.
   *There was so much food that I couldn't eat it all.*

Remember that *food* is an uncountable noun, so we have to use *much.* We also have to make the main verb and the pronoun singular. So be careful in the following examples.

4. After the chicken, she gave me a whole dishful of apples and bananas.
   There .................................. I couldn't .........................................
   *There was so much fruit that I couldn't eat it all.*

5. After the fruit, she gave me a whole plateful of sandesh and rasagula.
   There ........................................................................................................
   ........................................ .
   *There were so many sweets that I couldn't eat them all.*

6.  Last night I had to mark exam. scripts, correct essays, prepare my lessons, write this chapter. There ..............................................................
    ...................................................... .
    *There was so much work that I couldn't do,* or *finish, it all.*

7.  My students asked me about life in England, about the food, the weather, the people, the colour prejudice. There ................................
    ............................................................................
    *There were so many questions that I couldn't answer them all.*

8.  Oedipus asked me how many cows and bulls and bullocks there were in the field. But there..................................................................................
    ............................................ .
    *There were so many cattle that I couldn't count them all.*

Did you remember that *cattle* doesn't take a final *s* although it is a plural collective noun? Be careful.

9.  My host wanted to introduce me to all the men and women in the room. But ......................................................................................
    ....................................
    *There were so many people that I couldn't meet them all.*

In the next drill, a hyponymous relationship is exploited between adjectives and abstract nouns.

(ii) How about this red dress, madam?
     No....*I would prefer a different colour.*

It's a very soft material.
Yes....*I like its texture.*

It's charmingly striped and polka-dotted.
No....*I would prefer a different pattern.*

It's full-skirted and short-sleeved.
Yes....*I like its style.*

This oval handbag matches it beautifully.
Yes....*I like its shape.*

I can let you have them both for 2 pounds.
Oh, in that case....

This drill is contrasting the conditional and present tense of the verbs like *like* and *prefer.* The next example reverts to the perfect tense through a series of locative hyponyms.

(iii)

Is this your first visit to London?
*Yes, I've never been to England before.*

Is this your first visit to the British Museum?
*Yes, I've never been in London before.*

> Is this your first visit to Paris?
> *Yes, I've never been to France before.*

> Is this your first visit to the Louvre?
> *Yes, I've never been in Paris before.*

> Is this your first visit to the moon?
> *Yes, I've never been in space before.*

> Is this your first visit to the Copernicus Crater?
> *Yes, I've never been on the moon before.*

This drill could be extended in time, as well as in space, to cover other destinations, other uses of prepositions, and other occurrences of articles in place names. But here we shall journey no further into hyponymy. We shall only note in passing that hyponymy drills are not reversible. We cannot interchange prompt and response, for the simple reason that the transition from the general to the particular is less predictable than that from the particular to the general. We can expect a student to know that red is a colour, and can therefore use the first term in a drill to prompt the second. But we can't predict what colour he will name if we start from the more general term. Synonymy drills, and the remaining kinds of drill we shall now study, can be reversed. Responses can be interchanged with prompts and in some cases we can profitably derive two drills from one set of examples.

## 8 Antonymy drills

The next drill shows antonymous relationships being developed mainly between verbs:

(i) The other day my friend Harold decided to get married.
   *Why didn't he stay single?*

   Because he had met this beautiful girl. But his plan failed.
   *Why didn't it succeed?*

   Well, he proposed to her but she refused.
   *Why didn't she accept?*

   Because she said her father had forbidden it.
   *Why didn't he permit it?*

   Because he hates Harold.
   *Why doesn't he like him?*

   Because Harold supports Rangers and he supports Celtic. You do know that Celtic lost the cup last year?
   *Why didn't they win?*

   Because they played on the defensive all the time.
   *Why didn't they attack?*

I don't know. Anyway, Harold is still full of hope.
*Why doesn't he despair?*

Because Celtic are bound to win the cup this year.

The drill presupposes a certain amount of local knowledge about Scottish football teams. It also practises the formation of negative questions. The next drill reverts to the perfect tense, by relating nouns antonymously to verbs:

| | |
|---|---|
| (ii) Harold is still a bachelor. | *He hasn't got married yet.* |
| His girlfriend is still a spinster. | *She hasn't got married yet.* |
| Trofimov is still a student. | *He hasn't graduated yet.* |
| Felicity is still a schoolgirl. | *She hasn't left school yet.* |
| Anthony is still a child. | *He hasn't grown up yet.* |
| Are you still at school? | |
| Are you still a student? | |
| Are you married? | |

The next drill converts adjectives into abstract nouns:

| | |
|---|---|
| (iii) Pala isn't a rich country. | *There's still a lot of poverty.* |
| Pala isn't a healthy country. | *There's still a lot of disease.* |
| Pala isn't a progressive country. | *There's still a lot of reaction.* |
| Pala isn't a socialist country. | *There's still a lot of capitalism.* |
| Pala isn't a law-abiding country. | *There's still a lot of lawlessness.* |
| Pala isn't an industrial country. | *There's still a lot of agriculture.* |
| Pala doesn't allow free entry. | *There are still a lot of restrictions.* |

The final example contrasts antonymous prepositions:

| | |
|---|---|
| (iv) Are you standing up? | *No, I'm sitting down.*[5] |
| Is your tape going backwards? | *No, it's going forwards.* |
| Is Anthony getting up? | *No, he's staying in bed.* |
| Is Felicity staying at home? | *No, she's going out.* |
| Did the Light Brigade charge down the valley? | *No, they charged up the valley.* |
| Were there cannon to the left of them? | *No, there were cannon to the right of them.* |
| Have we got this the right way round? | *No, we've got it the wrong way round.* |

The early examples here practise the present continuous tense. The alternation of prepositions leads us straight into the first example of a new kind of implication relationship:

## 9  Converse drills

(i) The cat is on the mat.      *So, the mat is under the cat.*
The letter *e* comes before *i*.    *So, the letter* i *comes after* e.
The river goes under the bridge. *So, the bridge goes over the river.*
Who is sitting on your left in
the laboratory?               *X is.*
So, you...                   *So, I am sitting on X's right.*
Who is sitting on your right?    *Y is.*
So, you....                  *So, I am sitting on Y's left.*
Who did you say was sitting
on either side of you?         *X and Y.*
So, you...                   *So, I am sitting between X and Y.*
Who is sitting in front of you? *Z is.*
So, you...                   *So, I am sitting behind Z.*
Who is sitting behind you?     *O is.*
So you...                    *So, I am sitting in front of O.*

The greater part of this drill is open-ended. The responses indicate what a student might say. X and Y can of course stand for any real person or for nobody. The pairs of prepositions in prompt and response are antonymous. But the sentences in which they appear are synonymous because the order of the constituents has been reversed. The sentences are thus in *converse* relationship. Converse relationships may be created by verbs as well as by prepositions.

(ii)  Are you going to lend Harold the money?
*He's already borrowed it from me.*

Are you going to sell Stirling the car?
*He's already bought it from me.*

Are you going to rent your house to them?
*They've already rented it from me.*

Converse relations also hold between adjectives in the comparative degree:

(iii) Delhi is a little colder than Calcutta.
*Calcutta is a few degrees hotter than Delhi.*

Brutus is a little heavier than Cassius.
*Cassius is a few pounds lighter than Brutus.*

Anthony is a little shorter than Felicity.
*Felicity is a few inches taller than Anthony.*

In winter the days are a little shorter than in summer.
*In summer the days are a few hours longer than in winter.*

Father is a little older than mother.
*Mother is a few years younger than father.*

The paperback edition is a little cheaper than the hardback.
*The hardback edition is a few pence more expensive than the paper-back.*

Sophia Loren is a little more beautiful than my girlfriend.
*My girlfriend is a little less beautiful than Sophia Loren.*

This drill practises the use of plural nouns after *a few*, and a few anomalies in the use of comparative adjectives. *More expensive* is an alternative to *dearer*. And *uglier* would be inappropriate in the last example. Beauty, as this example incidentally shows, is a quality that cannot be quantified.

The next drill exploits conversely paired nouns.

(iv) Is that your girlfriend?          *No, I don't know who her boyfriend is.*

    Is Zarina your secretary?      *No, I don't know who her boss is.*

    Is Sophia Harold's wife?       *No, I don't know who her husband is.*

    Is Felicity your god-child?    *No, I don't know who her godfather is.*

    Is Oedipus your child?         *No, I don't know who his parents are.*

    Is Frankenstein your patient?  *No, I don't know who his doctor is.*

    Is Cerberus your dog?          *No, I don't know who its owner is.*

The drill is concerned with indirect speech and word order once again. The converse relationship is not quite so plain. But supposing I were Sophia's husband, it follows conversely that she is my wife.

## 10 Consequence drills

The state of marriage is a consequence of the act of getting married, and it produces its own consequences. It has its exits and its entrances. Entering, exiting from, and being in, a state can all be related by *consequential* implications. Consequential relations between verbs and adjectives are exploited in the next drill:

(i) The cat has been killed.          *It is now dead.*

    Frankenstein's monster has
    escaped.                      *He's now free.*

    Harold has got what he wanted. *He's now content.*

    I've eaten all I can.          *I'm now full.*

    Samson has lost his sight.     *He's now blind.*

    Lear has lost his senses.      *He's now mad.*

    Jim is losing his hair.        *He's becoming bald.*

The last example suggests an extension of the drill to contrast things that you can become and things that you are. You can't become dead, for example, though you can both be and become deaf.

(ii) Sophia is married now.      *She's become a wife.*
Clytemnestra has lost her
husband.      *She's become a widow.*
Harold has been elected now.      *He's become an M.P.*
Celtic have won the cup.      *They've become champions.*
Clement has been ordained
now.      *He's become a priest.*
Jim has changed his religion.      *He's become an apostate.*
MacHeath has been captured
now.      *He's become a prisoner.*

In this drill, verbal events have nominal consequences:

(iii)

Grgic is a good chess player.
*He's such a good player that he always wins.*

Jim is a bad player.
*He's such a bad player that he always loses.*

An elephant has a good memory.
*It has such a good memory that it never forgets.*

Macbeth invited us to a dull banquet.
*It was such a dull banquet that we were all bored.*

Mercutio told us a funny story.
*It was such a funny story that we all laughed.*

Jacques told us a sad story.
*It was such a sad story that we all cried.*

Adjectival states can also lead to verbal consequences:

(iv) Your hair is too long.      *You must get it cut.*
Your watch is broken.      *You must get it repaired.*
Your trousers are creased.      *You must get them pressed.*
Your shirt is torn.      *You must get it mended.*
Your suit is stained.      *You must get it cleaned.*
The petrol tank is empty.      *You must get it filled.*
The dog licence has expired.      *You must get it renewed.*

This drill could practise the use of *faire faire* in French. [6]
Verbs can, of course, enter into consequential relationships with other verbs:

(v) John is still climbing the mountain.
*He hasn't reached the top yet.*

Mother is still looking for her key.
*She hasn't found it yet.*

Felicity is still chasing the cat.
*She hasn't caught it yet.*

Rip Van Winkle is still sleeping.
*He hasn't woken up yet.*

John and Mary are still only engaged.
*They haven't got married yet.*

Peter is still studying for his degree.
*He hasn't graduated yet.*

This example completes my illustration of meaningful structural drills. In the next section we shall look at meaningful pronunciation practice before discussing the limitations of both types of meaningful drill.

# I I  Meaningful pronunciation drills

In the previous chapter, a selection of meaningless pronunciation drills was illustrated. The drills in this chapter have all practised pronunciation incidentally, and the application drills do so meaningfully. Attention could be further focused on pronunciation difficulties through the different kinds of applicational prompt. Pictures, for instance, of the relevant objects could prompt the student to distinguish between the vowel sounds in words such as *ship* and *sheep*, *cup* and *cap*, *cat* and *cart* — always assuming he could name the objects depicted. The identification of relevant sound effects might even lead to his producing the consonantal contrasts in *mouse* and *cows*, *ship* and *sip*, *breathe* and *breeze*. Here I shall only illustrate one meaningful pronunciation drill. It demands variation in the rhythm and in the intonation of a sentence. It uses a combined pictorial and verbal prompt. The prompt indicates which of the five syllables in the sentence is to be the tonic syllable. The first example shows a normal placing of the tonic, the remainder show different kinds of emphasis. The student looks at the picture and hears a comment from someone who is apparently hard of hearing. The student patiently replies, reading his answers aloud.

| | |
|---|---|
| What's that? | *It's a pencil.* |
| It isn't a pencil. | *It is a pencil.* |
| Did you say pensell? | *No, it's a pencil.* |
| Did you say "the pencil"? | *No, it's a pencil.* |
| So she's a pencil? | *No, it's a pencil.* |

Collocation and implication relationships can also prompt words differing in sound or stress like *ship* and *sheep*, *blackbird* and *white sheep*. One traditional way in which they may do so is through children's riddles. But to illustrate these here would be to encroach on the territory of comprehension exercises.

## 12   Drills as tests

In the discussion of what various meaningful drills do, I have used the words *illustrate, elicit, reveal, practise* and *test* interchangeably. It is now relevant to enquire what the drills illustrate, elicit etc. Is it simply sounds, as was argued in the case of meaningless drills, or structures and meanings as well? Let me take the last two terms *practise* and *test* first, and draw a distinction between them. Assuming for the moment that meaningful drills do practise structures, we have seen that they continuously test the student's knowledge of meaning relationships. While the structure may remain the same throughout the drill, each new prompt requires the student to adjust the vocabulary of the sentence in a relevant way. Four variables thus appear in the drill!:

1. The nature of the prompt.

2. The nature of the response.

3. The length of the prompt.

4. The length of the response.

The nature of the prompt, or rather of the meaning relationship between prompt and response, can be varied at will, within the same drill, without affecting the structural nature of the response.

(i) How do you get drunk?       *By drinking too much.*
How do you see the world?     *By travelling.*
How can you get to India most
quickly?                    *By flying.*
How do people earn their
living?                    *By working.*
How does a baker earn his
living?                    *By making bread.*
And a grocer?            *By selling provisions.*
And a taxi-driver?       *By driving a taxi.*
And your English teacher?   *By teaching English.*
And Georges Simenon?     *By writing detective stories.* [7]

The successive prompts test the student's knowledge of consequences, of the world, of collocation, and of derivational processes. Provided his knowledge is not at fault, he may not even notice the variations in the prompt. This allows us to set up a general principle for the design of drills. There is no need to keep meaning relationships pure, as I have tried to do in my examples for the sake of clarity. The only limitations on the variation and choice of prompts are empirical: Do they give the student a fair chance of producing utterances of the required structural type?

The same principle does not hold in the same way for the responses. If we vary the structural nature of the response beyond narrow limits, we are testing the student's knowledge of structural rules rather than giving him a chance to consolidate his knowledge. In many of my examples I have varied the response deliberately and I have done this for several reasons. I wanted to show how one drill might lead into another. I wanted to teach the student when not to use a particular structure. And I wanted to keep the student alert. Doubtless many of the drills could be improved or simplified as practice materials by eliminating the anomalous responses. But there comes a point — the fourth stage of teaching, to be precise — when we want to test the student to see what he has learnt. One form of test is something that looks like a drill but that requires continual variation in response:

(ii) *See if you can use the right part of the verb* to be *with the four phrases* so much, so many, so little, so few *and appropriate countable or uncountable nouns in the following passages:*

1. There...............................that we can't staff all the hospitals. There ............... that there isn't enough room for all the patients. There..............................that they can't all be given beds. There ..............................that we can't buy all the necessary drugs.

2. There..............................that many people are unemployed. For each vacancy, there ...............................that not all of them can be interviewed.

3. The monsoon failed last year. There ..................................... that the crops would not grow. There ..................................... that the wild animals were dying of thirst. There.............................. .................. who were starving that the government had to send relief. The year before there ..............................that the fields were flooded.

(iii) *Answer these questions with complete sentences:*

1. Must I have a visa to come to England?

2. Must I have a passport?

3. Need I register with the police if I only stay for two months?

4. And if I change my mind and stay for six months?

5. If I change my address after that, what happens?

6. Must I have a licence to drive a car?

7. Must I have a British licence?

8. How do I get a British licence?[8]

(iv) *Read the following passage carefully. Then complete the seven sentences beneath. Complete the sentences by writing the word* thermometer *or* thermometers *and by adding* the, some *or* some of the *if an article is needed.*

John wants to measure the temperature of a liquid. He hasn't got a

Fahrenheit thermometer in his laboratory. He has two kinds of Centigrade thermometer. One kind contains mercury and the other kind contains alcohol. He chooses a mercury thermometer because the liquid has a very high boiling point.

1. ............................... are used to measure temperature.

2. ............................... work on the Fahrenheit scale.

3. ............................... measure in Centigrade.

4. ............................... in John's laboratory are all on the Centigrade scale.

5. ............................... in his laboratory contain alcohol.

6. ............................... in his laboratory contain mercury.

7. ............................... John used contained mercury.

The three sample tests vary as much in style as in content. Test (iii) (on *mustn't, needn't* etc.), could be performed entirely on the radio. It requires complete sentences from the student. Tests (ii) and (iv) need written prompts since they employ a blank-filling technique. The student could, of course, record his answers on the tape.

The final test on the use of determiners includes also a fairly long introductory passage. It thus increases the length of the prompt since an understanding of the passage is material to the production of correct responses. If the passage were recorded rather than written, it would test the student's oral comprehension. Lengthening the prompt in prose, or in verse in the case of riddles, effects a transition from drill to comprehension exercise. Lengthening and varying the response effects a transition from drill to production exercise. Exercises, as we shall see in the next two chapters, are extended, and continually varying, kinds of test. They test the student's knowledge of meaning relationships as well as his knowledge of structural and phonological rules. How far can meaningful drills be said to practise the same?

## 13  Review of drills

Let us first briefly review the possible forms and various ambitions of drills.

1. *Meaningless drills* employ either cue words or whole sentence prompts to:

    (i) substitute new vocabulary items in a sentence;
    (ii) mutate, or change, the form of certain of its constituents;
    (iii) transform the sentence type by adding, deleting, permuting, or replacing constituents.

2. *Meaningful drills* substitute, mutate and transform by appealing to:
    (a) application relationships, prompted by

Collocation = to group words together in some system or order

(i) pictures;

(ii) sound effects;

(iii) knowledge of the world;

(b) collocation relationships between vocabulary items in a sentence (involving any or all of its constituents), prompted by cue words or whole sentences;

(c) implication relationships between sentences, prompted by whole sentences and requiring the substitution of

(i)  synonyms;

(ii)  hyponyms;

(iii)  antonyms;

(iv)  converse terms;

(v)  consequences in place of their antecedents.

Each and every type of drill may

(a)  elicit sentences of a single structural type;

(b)  contrast two structures;

(c)  test two or more structures, either diagnostically to find out whether the student needs to do a particular set of drills, or as a post-mortem to see if he needs to do them again.

Each and every type of drill may

(a)  elicit unrelated sentences from the student;

(b)  build up something that begins to look like connected spoken prose.

Each and every type of drill may be presented in programmed or in drill format.

I have illustrated meaningful drills at some length in the preceding sections for several reasons. Their nature and scope is less familiar than that of meaningless drills. Consequently their performance is largely untested. They are an untried weapon in the war against mistakes. But they are extremely flexible. I have shown that the same structural point (the perfect tense) can be approached in at least 15 different kinds of meaningful drill (counting those that can be worked backwards). I have also illustrated a number of other structural points to make it clear that meaningful drills can cover as extensive a range of syntactic problems as can meaningless drills. The question which must now be tackled is whether they also suffer from the same limitations.

## 14  The liability of errors

They certainly do not prevent the learner making mistakes. He is now invited to produce both grammatical and semantic errors. And the way to the latter is left wide open because meaningful prompts, unlike structural ones, do not generally suggest a single right answer. In my examples, for instance, I have sometimes had to indicate acceptable variants, and you may have thought of many other alternative readings. We can be reasonably sure that in the heat of the drill students will produce still further alternatives, acceptable or otherwise, which we would never have predicted. Let us just consider some possible responses to a single prompt in a drill eliciting a single structure:

Do you want this book?                *I've already read [ri:d] it.*
                                      *I've already heard it.*
                                      *I've already looked through it.*
                                      *I've already inwardly digested it.*

Only the third of these responses is acceptable. The rest illustrate formal, collocational and stylistic infelicities. We can eliminate from our drills prompts that leave the door too wide open, but we cannot close the door completely without shutting out meaningful prompts altogether. An alternative is to list on the tape all conceivable acceptable answers. But this would merely slow down proceedings without doing much good. The student who produces the third response above would be satisfied, but the others might still be mystified. We must remember the difference between knowing the right answer and merely becoming acquainted with it. The student who makes the first mistake may not know why or even whether he was wrong, assuming he notices the difference between what he said and what he subsequently hears. The students who made the second and fourth mistakes are still in the dark about whether their versions are acceptable alternatives. There is only one effective remedy. Call – or, in some American laboratories, dial – the teacher. In so far as meaningful drills encourage such consultation on a wide range of mistakes and alternatives, this seems to me to be to their credit. Once the student has consulted the teacher about any deviant responses, he can always be asked to do the drill again to practise the response we intended. A good test of a drill is whether a student can profitably do it twice.

## 15  Are meaningful drills structural?

In the previous chapter, it was argued that the tum-te-tum effect might render traditional drills both meaningless and structureless. Meaningful drills are not free from the same effect, though they may escape the first consequence. The second can be put to the test by asking the reader to do another Bengali drill under the same conditions as before. The drill is supposedly contrastive. Study the vocabulary list first, then refer to it as often as you need in the course of doing the drill:

*am* = mango, *phol* = fruit
*alu* = potato, *torkari* = vegetable
*shondesh* = kind of sweet, *mishti* = sweet
*rojoni gondha* = tuberose, *phul* = flower
*uils* = a brand of *sigaret*

*choti* = sandal, *juto* = footwear
*torch* = a kind of *bati* (light)
*jire* = a kind of *moshla* (spice)

The drill reflects a series of conversations between a foreigner and
various Bengali shopkeepers. The foreigner is beset by the problem of all
strange countries, finding out which shops sell what things:

| *Foreigner* | *Shopkeeper* |
|---|---|
| ami am chai. | *kintu amar phol nei.* |
| ami alu chai. | *bhalo, amar torkari achhe.* |
| ami shondesh chai. kintu.. | *amar mishti nei.* |
| ami rojoni ghonda chai. bhalo.... | *amar phul achhe.* |
| ami uils chai. kintu... | *amar sigaret nei.* |
| ami choti chai. bhalo... | *amar juto achhe.* |
| ami torch chai. bhalo... | *amar bati achhe.* |
| ami jire chai. kintu... | *amar moshla nei.* |

You may have guessed, from my description of the context, something
of what this means. The foreigner is saying:

I X want. (I want a, or some, X.)

The shopkeepers say:

But of me Y exists not. (But I don't have any Y.)
Good, of me Y is. (That's fine, I've got all kinds of Y.)

You can produce these variations in response quite correctly as soon as
you realise where the superordinate term for the noun in the prompt is to
be inserted in the response. The drill does not require you to realise that
*ami* and *amar* are nominative and possessive forms of the same pronoun,
that possessive relationships can only be expressed in Bengali through the
use of the verb *to be* together with a noun in the possessive case, or that
there are other ways of saying *be* in Bengali, but only this one is appropriate here. In other contexts where we would say *be,* quite different verbs
would be used, or no verb at all.

## 16   Are meaningful drills meaningful?

Meaningful drills, like meaningless drills, only provide positive examples.
They thus run the same risk of encouraging the student to overgeneralise.
At the same time, the tum-te-tum effect makes it possible for the student
not to generalise at all, but to perform the drill mechanically. To the
extent that this is true, meaningful drills may not practise structures
either. A further doubt arises: How far are meaningful drills meaningful to
the student? Does he either mean what he says or say what he means? We
must distinguish between several meanings of meaning:

**1. Applicational meaning,** or the conventional relationship between a word and the things to which it refers, between a sentence and the situations to which it is applicable.

**2. Implicational meaning,** or what a particular utterance necessarily entails (cp. the cat's and the mat's positions respective to each other).

**3. Collocational meaning,** which determines whether or not an utterance is significant, whether it is sensical or non-sensical (cp. the White Queen in *Alice*).

**4. Factual implications and consequences:** these have so far only been touched upon in connection with what road signs signify (cp. drill 5.1 (v)).

**5. Intended meaning:** this relates to the speaker's purpose or intention in making a particular utterance: *"The cat's on the mat again,"* might be a simple observation of facts, or a request to the hearer to remove either cat or mat.

**6. Attitudes:** We very often reveal our attitudes to what we are saying by the way we say it. The remark about the cat, for instance, could be made angrily, reproachfully, deiightedly, or sorrowfully.

Only the first four of these types of meaning can be said to be practisable in the laboratory. Drills either test or teach the semantic structures and systems of the language grouped under the headings of implication and collocation. They either test or teach knowledge of the world and of the local culture whose language the student is learning. They may not do any of this systematically, but to attempt it is surely better than nothing. That they do so at all is only because they allow the student some choice. He has no similar choice about conveying his own intentions or attitudes. But if we pre-ordain the intentions and attitudes that the student is to adopt, his utterances are bound to remain purposeless, and to this degree meaningless. He is not saying what he means, but only what we want him to say.

Think what might happen if the student were allowed to determine his own intentions and responses. When we ask him:

Would you like this book?

prompting a response of agreement in the perfect tense, any free and rational soul would respond:

What book?

thus initiating in real life an interesting conversation about the speaker's and the hearer's attitudes to the book or to literature in general.

Of course, we have a purpose in getting him to respond our way, and he may both discern our purpose and imagine that he is pursuing his own, which is to learn to talk. But an honest appraisal of his responses must lead to the conclusion that he is practising structurespeech, not communication, and structurespeech without much emphasis on structures. The intelligent student, no doubt, may appear to learn a lot from them. But it is the intelligent student who will learn from almost any form of exposure to the language, from studying a grammar book or reading novels as much as from drills. The advantage of drills over novels is that they give intensive experience of the spoken form of the language, though this could also be obtained through simple listening practice. The advantage of drills over a grammar book is that they give more extensive examples and may thus help the student to remember a rule through repetition. But it is up to the student to perceive the rule in the examples. We have seen that a drill does not always make it necessary for him to do so. It is also up to the student to find a use for the rule outside the drill situation. By eliminating or severely restricting the choice of structure, drills preclude genuine practice in conversation.

I have devoted a great deal of space to the scope and the limitations of drills in the last two chapters. My purpose was to distinguish between appearance and reality, in so far as we can approach reality by analysis or by appeal to results. Drills, it must be recalled, are the central means of practice in the behaviourist approach to language teaching. They fit into a view of language and of learning which at first seems both inclusive and convincing. Claims have been made on the basis of this approach that drill work in the laboratory will increase the effectiveness of instruction or should indeed replace all other forms of instruction. Teachers who have adopted this approach, however, are becoming increasingly dissatisfied with the results. The cause of this inadequacy lies not in faulty design, but in a basic misconception in approach. Because students appear to converse in a laboratory, it was too quickly concluded that they were practising talking. Because the drill appears to rehearse a structural pattern, it was thought that the student was acquiring control over structures. I have drawn a distinction between talking and structurespeech to make it clear that drills are in reality concerned with the latter. I have highlighted the tum-te-tum effect to show that in practice drills may be little more than exercises in pronunciation.

To some readers the space and effort devoted to establishing these points may seem disproportionate. All that has been discovered is that drills are not enough. But in the past drills have occupied the greater part of the student's time in the laboratory, and it seemed worth investigating what he might learn from them. Once the limitations of drills become apparent, the remaining chapters in this book assume their due importance. Can exercises and problems remedy the deficiencies of drills? In particular, can they focus the student's attention on grammatical structure and can they give him effective practice in talking? The value of the language laboratory as an aid to learning depends on the kind of answers we can give to these questions.

NOTES

1. J. Lyons: *Introduction to Theoretical Linguistics,* Cambridge University Press, 1968. I have taken all the terms I shall use for different kinds of meaningful drills from this book.

2. This drill was partly inspired by the British Council course, *The Turners.* It is one of the few published courses to use picture prompts. They are presented to the student in a little booklet which he takes with him into the laboratory.

3. This drill was inspired by a similar drill in French of Miss Dorothy Forrester's, as were examples 3 (i) on page 66 and 4 (i) on page 67.

4. This is not a nonsensical suggestion. Michael West suggests an ingenious "Read and Look Up" technique, by which the whole class can be got to read aloud at the same time. See: *Teaching English in Difficult Circumstances,* Longman, 1960.

5. This drill was stimulated by one of Miss Forrester's beginning: "Maman, je veux sortir." "Il faut que tu reste à la maison."

6. Some of the examples are borrowed from Miss Forrester.

7. This drill is adapted from a French one of Dorothy Forrester's, practising the use of *en* and a present participle.

8. This test is borrowed from Patrick Chaffey who originally designed it for Norwegian learners of English.

# 6 Comprehension exercises

*I have heard of thee by the hearing of the ear*
*But now mine eye seeth thee.*

— JOB

## I The nature of exercises

Drills are concerned with selected structures, exercises with selected activities. In a drill the student's attention is concentrated on giving a grammatically correct response. In an exercise, he has to find an appropriate and adequate answer. He may have to decide what other people's intentions and attitudes are, or to determine and express his own. The structural, phonological and lexical variations characteristic of an exercise reflect more fundamental variations in the character and purposes of speaker and hearer.

The purpose of a drill is to develop the student's competence, to practise and consolidate his knowledge of the rules of the language. Since such rules govern the formation of single sentences or the relationships between pairs of sentences, the unit of response in a drill is bound to be a single sentence prompted by another. The purpose of an exercise is to develop the student's repertoire of performance strategies. Exercises presuppose a certain knowledge of the linguistic rules, and they may also increase it. But their prime objective is to get the student to practise a skill. It might be note-taking, it might be composing an essay. The unit of response in an exercise can be longer or shorter than a single sentence. So can the prompt. The relationship between the two is one that, for want of a better term, I have called *factual implication*. When responses or prompts consist of more than one sentence, the succession of sentences displays logical or informational structure. Syntactic resemblances are incidental or for stylistic effect. The balanced parallelisms of the verses of the Bible, for instance, are not intended to drill the reader in substitution and transformation relationships.

Exercises involve activity. What kind of activity is suitable and purposeful for a particular learner? Why are the pupils learning the language? Notice that we cannot say "because they want to know the syntactic and semantic rules of the language". We certainly want them to speak correctly and with a good accent, but to what end? In the primary school we could probably say that ends and means are both enjoyment. We can make a virtue of felicity. But language learning in secondary schools and above is a more serious business. It involves essays, summaries, translation and textual criticism. All these demand purposeful and integrated activity on the part of the learner.

The exercises we design in the classroom and the laboratory should, then, correspond to the needs and purposes of the learner. The kinds of texts we use as prompts should contain the kind of language he needs to learn or study, whether it is literary or scientific, commercial or conversational. The kinds of activity in which the texts involve him should develop the skills he needs to learn and employ, whether these are critical or constructive, profitable or agreeable.

## 2  Types of exercise

Exercises can be classified according to the specific purposes they fulfil. A classification based on purpose will, of course, be far less precise than one based on types of linguistic rule. Rules are forthright and fixed, purposes are more elusive. Our explicit knowledge of linguistic rules is far greater than our ability to describe what is involved in successful performance. Nevertheless, we can look for suggestive labels. The two most obvious ones are *comprehension* and *production.* The distinction between the two is by no means absolute, but it does reflect a difference in purpose. The purposes of speaker and listener are seldom the same, though they may be complementary.

## 3  Comprehension exercises

Comprehension exercises themselves have two major purposes:

1. The student is intended to understand a text.

2. The student is made to show that he has understood.

These are not the same. It is the presence of the second activity that distinguishes comprehension exercises from the simple listening practice discussed in Chapter 3. Moreover, the achievement of the second aim does not test the achievement of the first, though it usually depends on it. I have hitherto talked of "testing understanding" or "misunderstanding". It is never in fact possible to do this directly. An element of willingness or wilfulness intervenes. The learner may wilfully misunderstand our questions, though he has understood the text. Or he may over-willingly answer our questions but, for one reason or another, fail to show that he has understood the text. Comprehension questions test his understanding or misunderstanding of the questions as much as of the text or anything else. This suggests a third purpose for comprehension exercises:

3. The student must be trained to infer the most likely sense of questions on the text.

This aim, and the second one, can only be achieved by obtaining active responses from the learner. Comprehension exercises thus involve, and become entangled in, the problem of production, just as production exercises involve, and become entangled in, the problems of comprehension. The principal object of the comprehension exercise remains that of obliging the student to select or manifest the most appropriate interpretation of something he has heard. Whereas the object of production is to get him to convey his own meaning.

## 4 Types of comprehension exercise

The prompt of a comprehension exercise may be any spoken text, from a single sentence to a long passage, in prose or in verse. It may be descriptive, narrative, conversational or instructional, with or without illustrations and sound effects.

The student's response, or reactions, to it may involve one or more of several different kinds of activities:

1. Answering questions.

2. Taking notes.

3. Making a summary.

4. Writing the passage (or parts of it) down i.e. dictation.

5. Following instructions.

Each of these constitutes a different type of exercise and will be illustrated separately.

## 5 Answering questions

This is an activity in which all of us engage, whether we are teachers or learners. Its practice in the laboratory, therefore, needs no further justification. But there is one difference, which should not be forgotten, between the way in which a teacher answers questions and the reason why a learner often has to do so. The teacher answers questions to supply relevant information to the ignorant and needy. The teacher asks questions to find out whether they have heard and understood. He is not generally concerned with *what* the learners tell him, but *whether* they can tell him. We should not follow this strategy too faithfully in the laboratory or we will miss an important point.

Exercises always have a double function. On the one hand they are concerned with the manifestation of a linguistically appropriate response, just as drills are concerned with correct responses. On the other hand, they teach learning and performance strategies. Exercises are techniques of teaching which attempt to teach techniques of learning. From this point of view, what matters is not only whether the learner can produce an acceptable answer in grammatical English, but also whether he has learnt to ask himself relevant questions. It will not be of much benefit to him if he can only answer our questions when he meets a real life text without any such guides. The higher achievement is to think of the right questions, not to know the right answers.

## 6  Asking questions

This sets the teacher in the laboratory a difficult but interesting task. He must so organise his own questions as to prompt the learner to notice what has not been questioned, and to formulate his own questions as well as his own answers. There are four techniques which the teacher may employ to do this:

1. True or false statements.

2. Blank-filling prompts.

3. Multiple-choice prompts.

4. Open-ended questions.

True or false questions are the simplest form of multiple choice. The learner has only to decide which of the two values applies to a particular statement, inference, or conclusion, or to answer a question with *yes* or *no*.

Blank-filling prompts suggest part of an answer to a question, which may involve citation from the text, a paraphrase of it, or inference and conclusions based upon it. Blank-filling prompts can organise responses through a linear programme, as has already been shown in the case of drills.

Multiple-choice prompts cover the same territory[1] and offer a further prospect. The alternative "answers" can be so arranged that each of the inappropriate ones anticipates a different kind of failure in the learner's control of language. Each wrong selection can then be followed up by appropriate remedial measures in the form of a branching programme. This will be illustrated in due course. Multiple-choice prompts that pay no heed to the learner's errors seem rather pointless. They tell the student when he is wrong and what the right answer should be, but they do not help him to find out why he was wrong.

Open-ended questions offer the learner no further guidance than the wording of the question. He is free to answer them as he wishes, and to formulate his own inferences, conclusions and further questions. Since his reactions are accordingly at their most unpredictable, it is impossible to build anything on them in the laboratory, or to organise them in the form of a programme. This does not mean that we should avoid open-ended questions in the classroom, or even in the laboratory. The open-ended question is after all the type we most frequently have to answer in real conversation. In the classroom we can check the student's answers as they are given. In the laboratory we can still give him practice in answering such questions, even if the teacher is not listening at the time. Since the answers can be recorded, they can always be checked later, though this will not always be possible in practice.

## 7 A lecture on linguistics

The first example of a comprehension exercise is artificially constructed to illustrate several kinds of listening problem. Ostensibly it is a lecture designed to teach the student or the reader something about linguistics. The lecture is continually interrupted by questions, both to check whether the student has been following and to train him in a listening strategy. A good listener is one who is always asking himself questions and anticipating what is going to be said next. Such a strategy is particularly valuable when the lecturer is allusive or obscure as this one is. The lecturer's words appear in roman type, and the comprehension questions in italic. The lecture is divided into numbered sections, each of which exemplifies different kinds of recognition problems.

**You are going to hear your first lecture on linguistics. I shall ask you questions in the course of the lecture. Stop the tape when you hear a question, think out your answer, and then record it. Here is the lecturer.**

(1)  "Linguistics is a science. . . ."

*What is the lecturer going to talk about, linguistics or science or both? . . . Well, you can be fairly sure he is going to talk about linguistics. That's the word he said first. But he may compare linguistics to other sciences. Let's see.*

"Linguistics is a science. Its first concern is to classify the data . . . "

*When the lecturer says "its first concern", what does it refer to, linguistics or science or both? . . . We can't refer to both or he would have used the plural pronoun* their. *Linguistics sounds like a plural noun but it's not. We decided that the lecturer was going to talk about linguistics so this is what it must be referring to. Let's listen again to what the first concern is.*

"Linguistics is a science. Its first concern is to classify the data. . . . "

*Does the word "data" mean* dates *or* facts *or something else?. . . . Data means facts, in this case the facts of language, linguistic facts. /ˈdeitə/ is the English way of pronouncing the Latin word spelt: d, a, t, a. Let's see if we are told what language data are.*

"The first concern of linguistics is to classify the data, the data of linguistic behaviour. Classification is made on the basis of distributional criteria . . . "

*What does this mean? . . . I don't know what you think it means but the lecturer hasn't explained it yet. Let's see if he does.*

"Classification is made on the basis of distribution. We can establish two different classes of words simply and only because they differ in distribution. Class 1 words occur in the environment:  following

The X is old.

Class 2 words occur in the environment:

It's very Y today. . . . "

*What are these Class 1 and Class 2 words? . . . You may not be able to guess yet, or you may not have guessed correctly. What do the words /eks/ and /wai/ mean? . . . X and Y are, of course, letters of the alphabet standing for different words.*

(2) "Given the environment 'It's very Y', we can now say. . . ."

*What does he mean when he says "given the environment"? Does somebody have to give us an environment? . . . No, an environment isn't a thing like a present that can be given to us. The word given here means "starting from something", "on the basis of something".*

"Given the environment 'It's very Y', we can now say that any words that occur in this environment, all words in fact that occur after 'very', are Class 2 words or what are traditionally called adjectives. . . ."

*Does he mean that they are either Class 2 words or adjectives? . . . No, he means that Class 2 words are the same as adjectives. We call them adjectives, he calls them Class 2 words. These are just two alternative names for the same thing.*

"And, given the environment 'The X is old', we can now say that words occurring in this environment are Class 1 words or nouns. There is no *a priori* reason to prefer one name to the other. . . ."

*How do you spell /ei praiɔrai/? . . . This is the English way of pronouncing two words, two Latin words. The first one consists of the letter* a, *and the second is spelt:* p, r, i, o, r, i. *Listen to what he says next if you don't know what it means.*

"There is no a priori reason, no theoretical or necessary justification, for calling them nouns rather than Class 1 words. Whichever name is used, distributional criteria must be established, or an important distinction may be ignored. . . . "

*Does he mean that we can ignore this distinction if we want to? . . . Of course not. If it is an important distinction we mustn't ignore it. He means that if we don't establish distributional criteria, we will be making a mistake.*

(3) "When traditional grammarians defined nouns, they defined them as the names of persons, places and things. This is quite a satisfactory definition if we already know which words are to be classified as nouns. . . ."

*Does the lecturer think that the traditional definition of a noun is quite satisfactory? . . . No, he doesn't. He means that if we don't*

already know which words are nouns, the traditional definition is
unsatisfactory.

*meanings criteria*

"Don't be deceived into thinking that semantic criteria can be used to
establish grammatical classes. . . . "

*Wait a moment. The lecturer has jumped a few steps of his argument
here. Does the traditional definition of a noun (as the name of a
person, place or thing) tell you anything about the environment in
which nouns may occur? . . . No. So what kind of definition is
it? . . . It's what the lecturer calls a semantic definition, it tells you
something about the meaning of nouns, but it doesn't tell you where
nouns may occur in a sentence, it doesn't define them by their environment. Does the lecturer think that semantic definitions can be
used to classify nouns? . . . No, listen to what he says.*

"I repeat, don't be deceived into thinking that semantic criteria and
definitions can be used to establish grammatical classes such as nouns
and adjectives. If we followed only the traditional definitions, *red*
would be a noun because it names a thing (a colour), while *courage*
would be an adjective because it names a quality. *Departure* and
*indignation* would both be verbs because they describe actions and
states, while *telephone* would be an adjective because it modifies the
noun *directory.*[2]

(4) "So we can see that the classical grammarians made a classical
mistake. Instead of looking for distributional criteria to establish
grammatical classes they counted their chickens before they were
hatched. . . ."

*Does he mean that classical grammarians counted chickens instead of
checking distributions? . . . No, of course not. "Counting your
chickens before they are hatched" is an idiom. It means anticipating
the results of an action too early.*

*structure*

"We need not follow them into this fallacy. Obviously, syntax is prior
to semantics, and therefore, to be scientific, we must start from the
distributional criteria without any prior assumptions."

*Why is syntax obviously prior to semantics? . . . The lecturer doesn't say.
Why must we start from the distributional data without any prior
assumptions? . . . The lecturer doesn't really explain why. He just states
that this is a scientific procedure. Is this what scientists really do? . . . No,
of course not. They always start from certain assumptions but they may
turn out to be the wrong ones. When the lecturer uses words like
obviously and* therefore, *he is really only telling you what he approves
of. Let's look at the word* fallacy *that he also used. He said . . .*

". . . in the traditional definition, a noun is the name of a person,
place or thing." *are nouns)*

*Is this a true account of the definition? . . . No, or at least not as it was originally formulated. The original definition goes: "Names of persons, places and things are nouns". Do these two definitions mean the same thing? . . . No. The statement "A cat is an animal" does not mean the same as "All animals are cats". Can you see the fallacy in the lecturer's arguments about how the definition applies to words like* courage, departure *and* indignation? *. . .*

*Well, the definition "A noun is the name of a person, place or thing" does mean that all nouns are names of one kind or the other. But the other definition, "Names of persons, places and things are nouns", allows us to decide that some words which are not the names of any of these may also be nouns. Does this mean the lecturer was wrong to stress the importance of distributional criteria? . . . No, he was only wrong in the reasons he advanced against semantic criteria. But he did make one mistake in his illustration of distributional criteria. Do you remember he said:*

". . . all words that occur after *very*, in the sentence 'It's very Y', are adjectives."

*Can you think of any words that can occur after* very *which are not adjectives? . . . Yes, of course, adverbs of manner like* quickly *or* brightly *can occur after* very *and before past participles. Incidentally adjectives like* principal, universal, *and* only *do not occur after* very.

## 8  Analysis of a lecture on linguistics

The first section of the lecture raises the problem of recognising what the speaker is talking about, both the general subject matter, and the successive topics that enter the discussion. The lecturer, for instance, introduces technical terms like *Class 1 word, distribution, environment,* without immediately explaining what they refer to. It may take the learner some time to realise that the distribution of a word is the sum of its environments.

The second section illustrates the problem of recognising how successive topics and statements about them are related to each other. The lecturer uses the relational conjunction *or* in two different senses, neither of which sets up disjunctive alternatives.

The third section reveals the problem of recognising the speaker's intentions. The lecturer uses the phrase *quite satisfactory* when he intends his listener to understand "satisfactory only under special conditions", and he makes the statement that semantic criteria are inadequate by means of an imperative: *"Don't be deceived into thinking. . . ."*

The fourth section illustrates the problem of recognising the speaker's attitude. In this example, the lecturer masks his feelings of approval and disapproval under the guise of a formal argument.

The final section of the exercise is concerned with the problem of recognising the overall logical and informational structure of a piece of discourse. In this case the exercise discloses gaps and fallacies in the argument, but it could lead on to the drawing out of implications, and their testing on further examples. The learner could, for example, be asked to suggest alternative distributional criteria for "catching" adjectives, or to anticipate what the lecturer would find unsatisfactory about the traditional definitions of verbs and adverbs.

All these are linguistic problems not in the narrow sense of being of concern only to the student of linguistics, but in the broadest sense that they are liable to confound or deflect all learners of a language at all stages. They are "very universal" problems, as anyone who has tried to follow an argument or instructions and directions in a foreign tongue will have learnt to his cost. In this exercise, the student's comprehension was tested with a series of open-ended and elementary multiple-choice questions. The latter kind of question was not used to exploit the student's possible mistakes. In the next exercise the multiple-choice form is developed into a remedial branching programme. Depending on which answer the student thinks is right, he is directed to different portions of the exercise.

## 9 The Secrets of the Grave — An exercise

**Listen to this bit of the story again:**    *Multiple Choice Qs.*

"Carter had discovered the entrance to a tomb. He had yet to find out whether there was anything inside. Stopping only to look for the missing torch, he made his way along the underground passage. At the end he found a door into a small room whose walls dimly reflected the light. In the middle of the room he saw, to his delight, a huge stone sarcophagus. When it was opened, he found himself staring into the face of a young man. The golden face stared back at him. He had found the last resting place of Tutankhamen. The ancient priests, whose records he had so patiently studied, had not lied when they told the story of this young king."

**Now stop your tape and answer the questions in your booklet.**

*Student's Booklet*

Which of the statements in this programme is right? Depending on which you choose, you will have to go to different frames. Follow the arrows.

1. (a) Carter had found out the entrance to a tomb.  —→   3

   (b) Carter had found the entrance to a tomb.  —→   6

2. (a) Carter had not yet found out if there was anything inside the tomb.  —→   5

    (b)  Carter had not yet found anything inside the tomb.   ⟶   7

---

3.  No. He hadn't "found out" the entrance to a tomb, he had found it. What's the difference between finding out something and finding something? Fill in the blanks with "found" or "found out":

    (1)  Carter later ............................ other rooms in the tomb.

    (2)  Carter later ............................ the other rooms in the tomb had been robbed.   ⟶   4

---

4.  (1)  He later found other rooms.

    (2)  He later found out they had been robbed.
        We talk about finding a thing that has been hidden, but finding out a fact that we did not know before.   ⟶   2

---

5.  Yes, Carter hadn't yet found out if anything was in the tomb.   ⟶   9

---

6.  Yes, Carter had found the entrance to a tomb.   ⟶   2

---

7.  No. It's true that he hadn't found anything yet, but then he hadn't yet looked inside the tomb. He wanted to find out if there was anything inside it. What's the difference between finding out something and finding something? Fill in the blanks with "find" and "find out":

    (1)  Carter wanted to ...................... the name of the King in the tomb.

    (2)  Carter wanted to ...................... the tomb of Tutankhamen.   ⟶   8

---

8.  (1)  He wanted to find out the name of the King in the tomb.

    (2)  He wanted to find Tutankhamen's tomb.

    We talk about finding out a fact that we didn't know before, but finding a thing that we are looking for.   ⟶   9

---

9.  (a)  Carter couldn't find a torch.   ⟶   12

    (b)  Carter managed to find out a torch.   ⟶   13

    (c)  Carter managed to find a torch.   ⟶   11 ✓

    (d)  Carter couldn't find out a torch.   ⟶   10

---

10.  No. He needed a torch to explore the tomb. The story talks about the walls of the room dimly reflecting its light. Does this mean:

    (a)  He had managed to find out a torch.   ⟶   13

(b) He had managed to find a torch. ⟶ 11

---

11. Yes. He managed to find a torch. The story tells you that the walls of the room dimly reflected its light. ⟶ 15

---

12. No. He did find a torch. The story talked about the walls of the room dimly reflecting its light. ⟶ 15

---

13. No. He hadn't "found out" a torch, he had found one. What's the difference between finding something and finding out something? Fill in the blanks with "found" or "found out":

    (1) At last I ..........................the money that I had lost.

    (2) At last I............................how much money I had lost. ⟶ 14

---

14. (1) I found the money.

    (2) I found out how much I had lost.

    We talk about finding a thing that is lost or missing, but finding out a fact that we didn't know before. ⟶ 15

---

15. (a) In the room, Carter found a stone sarcophagus. ⟶ 19 ✓

    (b) In the room, Carter found out a stone sarcophagus. ⟶ 17

---

16. (a) Carter had found Tutankhamen out. ⟶ 25

    (b) Carter had found out Tutankhamen. ⟶ 24

    (c) Carter had found Tutankhamen in. ⟶ 20

    (d) Carter had found Tutankhamen. ⟶ 22 ✓

---

17. No. He didn't "find out" the sarcophagus, he found it. A sarcophagus is a kind of box, or coffin, for putting bodies in. What's the difference between finding out something and finding something? Fill in the blanks with "found" and "found out":

    (1) Yesterday I ...........................I had won ten rupees in the lottery.

    (2) Yesterday I ...........................ten rupees in the street. ⟶ 18

---

18. (1) I found out I had won 10 rupees.

    (2) I found 10 rupees in the street.

    We talk about finding out an unexpected fact, but finding a thing somewhere unexpectedly. ⟶ 16

19. Yes, he found the sarcophagus in the room. A sarcophagus is a kind of box, or coffin, for putting bodies in. ⟶ 16 ✓

20. No. He didn't "find Tutankhamen in", although it's true that he found his body in the sarcophagus. What's the difference between finding someone in and finding someone? Fill in the blanks with "find him" or "find him in":

   (1) I looked everywhere for Carter, but I couldn't ...........................

   (2) I went to Carter's house, but I didn't .......................................
   ⟶ 21

21. (1) I couldn't find him.

   (2) I didn't find him in.

   We talk about finding someone we are looking for, but finding them in when we find them at home. Since Tutankhamen was dead, it sounds very strange if you say that Carter found him at home! So, you should have said:

   (a) Carter had found out Tutankhamen. ⟶ 24

   (b) Carter had found Tutankhamen. ⟶ 22

22. Yes, he had found the last resting place of Tutankhamen. ⟶ 23

23. You have now finished this set of questions. Start the tape and listen to the next bit of the story again.

24. No. He hadn't "found out" Tutankhamen, he had found him. We talk about finding out facts, but finding people or things. Could we also say:

   Carter had found Tutankhamen out.     (a) Yes ⟶ 25

   (b) No ⟶ 23

25. No. He hadn't "found Tutankhamen out", he had found him. What's the difference between finding somebody and finding somebody out? Fill in the blanks with "found him" or "found him out":

   (1) I visited the old priest's room, but I..............................................

   (2) I looked for the old priest, but I never ........................................

   (3) The old priest was cheating me, but I never...........................
   ⟶ 26

26. (1) I found him out.

    (2) I never found him.

    (3) I never found him out.

    We talk about finding someone we are looking for. Finding some-
    one out means two quite different things. It either means that we
    discover they are not at home, or that we discover they have been
    cheating, or making a pretence. Could we also say, in either case:

    I found out the priest.　　(a) Yes　⟶　27

    　　　　　　　　　　　　　(b) No　⟶　23

---

27. No. We only talk about finding out a fact that we didn't know before.
    A priest is not a fact, he's a person. Fill in the blanks with "found" or
    "found out":

    (1) Carter...................................the ancient priests had not been lying
    when they referred to the young king in their records.

    (2) Carter.......................... the records referring to the young king.
    　⟶　28

---

28. (1) He found out the ancient priests had not been lying.

    (2) He found the records.

    We talk about finding out a fact, but finding a thing that we are
    looking for somewhere. Could we also say: Carter found the
    ancient priests had not been lying.

    (a) Yes　⟶　29

    (b) No　⟶　29

---

29. Yes. We can also talk about finding a statement to be true. This means
    coming to the conclusion that it is true. Carter found, or found out,
    that the ancient records were true when:

    (a) He found out Tutankhamen.　⟶　24

    (b) He found Tutankhamen.　⟶　23

---

## 10 Analysis of the Secrets of the Grave

Five of the questions set major comprehension traps. The able student
selects five alternatives, checks them, and is out of the programme after a
short comprehension exercise. The remaining 19 frames are for the confused student or for those who guess blindly. These frames are intended to

help the student distinguish between the verbs *find* and *find out*. This is a lexical confusion, encouraged perhaps by the fact that *discover* may be a synonym for both verbs in many of their different senses. Comprehension exercises can, and must, handle problems of lexical implication as well as those of factual implication illustrated in the previous exercise. The student must learn that the same word does not always have the same meaning. In addition to the differing senses of *find* and *find out* exemplified in the programme, the student at some later stage will have to distinguish further uses of *find:*

(i) Thus we find that semantic criteria alone are inadequate.
(ii) I found Carter in poor health.
(iii) Carter was finding the heat intolerable.
(iv) I find Tutankhamen a silly sort of fellow.

The problem of polysemy, or multiple meaning, becomes acute in literary language, where lexical ambiguity may be intended. Thus T. S. Eliot's lines,

In my end is my beginning . . .                 *end = goal - object*
In my beginning is my end . . .

summon up a whole range of meanings for two simple everyday words.

## I I  Building up vocabulary recognition

Whether our students are concerned with poetry or not, developing their powers of comprehension involves three different kinds of vocabulary building:

1. Learning new words.

2. Learning new meanings for known words.

3. Recognising which known meaning, or meanings, are operative in a particular context.      *Contextual meanings*

When any of these aims are the exclusive concern of a comprehension exercise, or part of one, we can ask the student to guess the meanings of words either before or after he listens to the passage. But if he is to have a chance of guessing correctly, the context must be engineered. Many students in the last exercise, for instance, might have been able to guess what a sarcophagus is. It is clearly something made of stone which you find inside a tomb, which can be opened and which contains a dead body. The context supplied collocational information about the word. A picture would give applicational information. Implication relationships can be suggested by other kinds of contextualisation. For example, look at these sentences adapted from a novel written in a Welsh border dialect of English.[3]

(i) We started swiving, that is reaping, at the beginning of August.

(ii) The ollern trees that fringed the road dripped with yellow catkins.

(iii) She was not at all jimp. She was clumsy and thick-bodied.

(iv) Now for all he was so big, Huglet didna want to wrostle. He hiver-hovered over it a good bit, for he knew Kester was a right proper wrestler.

(v) You know me and Jancis have taken together in good sadness.

The first example suggests that *reaping* and *swiving* are synonymous. If we know the one, we can guess the meaning of the other.

The second example introduces a hyponymy relationship between *ollern* and *tree,* and if we know which trees in the Welsh marches have yellow catkins, we can narrow down the reference still further.

The third example suggests an antonymous relationship between *jimp* and the two adjectives in the next sentence. *Jimp,* here, means graceful or slender.

The fourth example implies that *hiver-hovering* is a consequence of not wanting to do something. The sentences also manifest a derivational relationship between *wrostling* and *wrestler.* The words *right* and *proper* in this example do not necessarily imply that Kester was a correctly behaved wrestler. The unusual collocation of *good* and *sadness* in the last example suggests that the whole phrase is to be taken as an idiom. But the lack of further context leaves the sense of the idiom indefinite.

These examples suggest some ways in which we can help a student to guess the meaning of a new word. When it first appears in a comprehension text, it can be associated with a synonym, an antonym, or a superordinate term. The student can be taught to look out for such clues, or to note unusual collocations that may indicate a familiar word is being employed in an unusual sense. Generally, vocabulary building can be worked into other types of exercise whenever necessary. Some new technical terms were introduced into the exercise on lecture comprehension. A few more appear in the following exercises on note-taking and summarising.

## 12 Note-taking and summarising

These two forms of exercise will be illustrated together. Both involve comprehension just as much as question-answering does. But they lead to a more co-ordinated response. They are therefore particularly concerned with the problems of recognising logical relationships between topics and of discerning the logical structure of a whole "text". Since they demand the replacement of the original words and structures of the text by symbols or paraphrases of the student's own choice, they also raise all the problems of factual and lexical implication.

Note-taking is an essential skill for any student intending to study in a foreign language. Summarising has an additional value as a means of organising what we learn in our own terms.

The following exercises were designed as part of a course for a group of overseas students newly arrived in Britain. They had been accepted for undergraduate or postgraduate courses, mainly in science and engineering. They had a good knowledge of technical or semi-technical vocabulary but a variable ability to understand lectures. Accordingly the texts used for note-taking are miniature versions of what the students will soon have to tackle. They hear small extracts from textbooks being read aloud and listen to recordings of very short lectures which exhibit all the features (hesitations, false starts, pauses, incomplete utterances etc.) of unscripted monologue. The note-taking symbols used are an extended and modified version of those taught in the Interpreters School in Geneva.[4] They are intended to be easy to use and easy to read back. Techniques of abbreviation are not illustrated in the exercises, though any student employing a consistent system could produce still shorter and more rapid notes.

## 13  Contrasts — An exercise

*In these exercises, you are going to learn to recognise and symbolise a new relationship between sentences. You have already learnt how to use the equals sign and various kinds of arrows to show causes and consequences. You also know how to use different kinds of underlining for emphasis, and a question mark to indicate possibility. Now we are going to study contrasts. Listen to these two sentences:*

(1)  John's bicycle hit a stone, but he didn't fall off.

(2) Although John's bicycle had hit a stone, he didn't fall off.

*Which word in each sentence indicates that something expected didn't happen? . . . Yes, the conjunctions* but *and* although *contrast what happens with what was expected to happen. They contrast one event with another, one fact with another, or one idea with another. Now write down on Page 1 of your booklet all the expressions you can think of that mean the same as* but *or* although, *and which could be used in the sentences about John not falling off his bicycle when it hit a stone. Start the tape again when you have finished writing them down. . .*

*Well, instead of* but, *we could say* however, nevertheless, nonetheless *etc. And instead of* although, *we could say* in spite of the fact that, despite the fact that *or simply* though. *Let's symbolise all the words and expressions that can replace* but *by the three letter word: b, u, t. And all the words or expressions that can replace* although *by the three letter abbreviation: t, h, o.*

*Exercise 1. Listen to the following sentences as many times as you like. On page 2 of your booklet, note down the symbol that expresses the relationship between different parts of the sentence. Don't write anything else. Put the appropriate symbol beside the number of the sentence. Be careful. Not all the sentences contain contrastive expressions.*

1. The poor nations are getting poorer, whereas the rich nations are getting richer.

2. This kind of measure only provokes discontent.

3. Primitive peoples are often reluctant to change their trading methods in spite of the fact that they are sufficiently advanced to adopt more convenient methods.

4. It would nevertheless be dangerous to conclude that oral contraceptives are harmless.

5. This statement conflicts with the truth.

6. No matter how poor a man may be, he should be allowed to retain his self-respect.

7. Reo-virus type 3 is apparently identical with one involved in plant disease.

8. It is important to remember, however, that the evidence permits an alternative explanation.

9. At Dagenham, too, despite Ford's assurance that no further dismissals would take place, uncertainty persists.

*Now turn to page 3 of your booklet to check your answers. Start the tape again when you have finished.*

Booklet page 3:

1. tho

2. → (results in, leads to)

3. tho

4. but

5. ≠ (is different from, not the same as)

6. tho

7. = (is the same as)

8. but

9. tho

*Exercise 2. This time try to take short but complete notes on each of the sentences you will hear. Listen to them as many times as you like. Write your notes on page 4 of your booklet.*

1. There is very little evidence about the effects of noise, though it has been known for a long time that intermittent noise is a great handicap for the worker.

2. We must contrast this, however, with the behaviour of mason bees, which is quite different.

3. In some cases the worm damages the eyes and blindness is not an uncommon sequel.

4. Although the quantity of work done by the workers in the specially sound-proofed room was not different from that done by workers in the normal room, the quality of their work was much higher.

5. But although all four of the maternally-deprived young monkeys appeared to have returned' to normal within a few days, they then regressed for a while.

6. It is possible for children to suffer from protein deficiency where there is no overall food shortage.

7. While it is true that women seem capable of undertaking all the jobs that men perform, in most cultures they do not normally do so.

*Now turn to page 4 of your booklet to check your answers.*

Booklet page 4:

1. evidence about effects of noise, tho <u>known</u> that intermittent noise = handicap for worker.

2. But ≠ behaviour of mason bees.

3. sometimes worm damages eyes & → blindness.

4. sound-proofing ↗ quality but not quantity of work.

5. tho all 4 motherless monkeys → normal in <u>days,</u> then ↙ for a while.

6. ? children ← protein deficiency tho no overall food shortage.

7. tho ? women do all men's jobs, in <u>cultures</u> not normal.

*Exercise 3. Now you will hear a short lecture on methods of building suspension bridges. While you are listening, look at the diagrams on page 5 of your booklet. Make short but complete notes on the same page. Listen to the lecture as many times as you like.*

"There are er two distinct methods of constructing a cable for suspension bridges . . . the wires of which the cable is composed may be twisted into strands the strands themselves being twisted together to form the completed cable . . . or they may um be spun separately and clamped together like this . . this method takes much longer for the simple reason that each wire has to be individually adjusted before clamping you can see this it in the diagram here . . . whereas yes you see this diagram the strands of twisted wire can be erected as units . . . provided of course they are not so heavy as to be unmanageable however on bridges with very long spans there are . . . certain advantages in the parallel clamped wires method of spinning the cable . . . ."

*Now turn to page 6 of your booklet to check your notes against the suggested version.*

Booklet page 6:

1. 2 methods of constructing cable for suspension bridge
   (i)   wires twisted → strands & strands twisted → cable
   (ii)  wires separately spun & clamped together

2. but (ii) takes longer ∵ each wire adjusted individually but ? twisted strands erected as units unless <u>heavy</u>

(∵ is the symbol for "because")

3. But (i) better for <u>long</u> spans

*Exercise 4. You will now hear another short lecture, this time on radio stars. The numerical figures mentioned in the lecture are on page 7 of your booklet. Make your notes on the same page.*

"Now I'm going to tell you a remarkable fact about radio stars . . . through optical telescopes they appear just as dim specks of light . . . to radio telescopes they appear very bright now why is this? . . . well they appear dim to us only because the because they are so far away . . . in fact they must be 100 times brighter than the brightest galaxy of 10,000 million stars yes yet they are 10,000 times smaller . . . now one of the earliest investigators of radio stars Reber he found that the radio signals were strongest from directions near the Milky Way on the other hand . . . he completely failed to detect any signals from bright stars or from other features visible in space . . . so despite the fact that the radio sources were in densely populated stellar regions . . . despite this . . . there were no particular visual objects to which the radio emissions could be ah attributed. . . ."

*Now turn to page 8 of your booklet to check your notes against the suggested version.*

Booklet page 8:

1. through optical telescopes, radio stars = dim but to radio telescopes = <u>bright</u>

2. dim ∵ <u>far away</u>.
in fact 100 X brighter than galaxy of 10,000 million stars, tho 10,000 X smaller.

3. Reber: radio signals strongest from Milky Way but ↚ bright stars tho radio sources in <u>populated</u> regions, not visible.

*Exercise 5. Keep your booklet open at page 8. I want you now to turn these notes into a summary of the lecture. Look at note 1. Without chang-ing the order of the topics, can you suggest a complete sentence that would give all the information in the note? Stop your tape-recorder if you want to think for a moment . . . Are you ready? All right, tell me the first sentence of your summary now . . .*

*Here is my version:*

(1) Through optical telescopes radio stars are (or appear) very dim, but to radio telescopes they are extremely bright.

*I'll say my version again and I want you to repeat it . . . Did you notice that we didn't need to use the articles* the *or* a *in the first sentence? Now let's do the same for the second note. It's rather long so we had better make two sentences out of it . . . Are you ready? Tell me your next two sentences . . .*
*Now listen to my version:*

(2) They are dim because they are very far away.

(3) In fact, they are 100 times brighter than a galaxy of 10,000 million stars, although they are 10,000 times smaller.

*Now try repeating my sentences . . . Did you notice that we had to say* a *galaxy? It's a singular noun and it needs an article. Now let's do the last note. Again we'll need more than one sentence. See if you can do it in two . . . Are you ready? Tell me your last two sentences. . . .*

*Here is my version:*

(4) Reber found (or discovered) that the radio signals were strongest from the Milky Way, but they were not coming from bright stars.

(5) Although the radio sources were in extremely densely populated regions, they were not visible.

*Now repeat my sentences . . . Did you notice that we had to use the definite article three times in these sentences? We talked about the* Milky Way, *the* radio signals, *the* radio sources. *Why must we use this article before the last two? . . . Well, because we've already mentioned radio stars, and the signals are particular signals coming from these particular sources.*

*You have now finished the tape. But there is one more thing I want you to write in your booklet. Look at your own notes on page 7 and then write down on page 9 your own summary of the lecture on radio stars. Don't forget to put in little words like* the *and* a *which you have left out in your notes. When you have finished, show your booklet to me. I want to find out if your notes and your summary are better than mine.*

## 14   Comments on the exercise on contrasts

The central notion underlying this approach to note-taking is that the number of ways in which successive topics or sentences in connected discourse can be "logically" related to each other is extremely limited, though these relationships may be expressed in many different ways. The relationships illustrated in the exercises were of consequence, equivalence and contrast. Subsequent exercises would deal with further relationships such as conditionality. Initially students may be confused by the variety of stylistic devices a speaker employs to link his topics and may miss the essential sense of what he is saying. The exercises therefore train the student to identify logical relationships and to record each with a single distinct symbol. It is hoped that such a listening strategy will be of value even when the student is not concerned with taking notes. The listener is in effect building up a simplified logical skeleton of what he is hearing.

To give the student time to identify the relationships, he is invited to listen to each example as many times as he wishes. Obviously he cannot do this in real life. But one of the notable advantages of the laboratory as a training device is that it does permit exact repetition. And in the laboratory each student can repeat something as much as he needs without disturbing the progress of the rest of the class.

The student was required to write down not just his notes but a summary of what he had heard. The purpose of the written summary was to provide a permanent record in a form easily consulted again by himself, supposing he is genuinely interested in radio stars, and easily checked by the teacher. The exercise in oral summarising served merely to rehearse him in the problems of converting notes back into prose.

Written prompts and responses were also used in the previous exercise on "finding" and "finding out". This had an additional technical reason behind it. The tape-recorder itself cannot cheaply or readily be adapted to fit the requirements of a branching programme. The essence of the latter is that different students should receive differential treatment according to their needs and abilities, even in the course of a single exercise. Since we are concerned in this chapter with aural comprehension exercises, not oral production, there can be no objection to the use of written responses and tests when these are appropriate and effective ways of getting the student to react to what he has heard.

## 15 Dictation exercises

A written response is the only appropriate response in a dictation exercise. Dictation, of course, involves more than an ability to spell words and punctuate sentences. For either skill to be practised the student must first correctly hear what he has to write down. To hear correctly he must overcome at least four recognition problems:

1. Recognition of distinctive sounds.

2. Identification of homophones.

3. Identification of words, phrases and sentences.

4. Identification of intonation patterns.

The first can be practised even at an elementary level by asking the student to write down words such as *it* and *eat, watched* and *washed, place* and *plays,* presented either in pairs or in a larger context. Which particular sounds a student is liable to misidentify or confuse will depend to some extent on his mother tongue.

The second skill can only be practised if homophonous pairs such as *led* and *lead* (the metal), *their* and *there, witch* and *which,*[5] are presented in a context which disambiguates them, e.g.

Which doctor is he?

He's a witch doctor, is he?

A sophisticated exercise on these lines might involve restoring in full written form the words indicated in rapid speech by the single phonemes /d/ or /dʒ/.

| | |
|---|---|
| D'you like cowboy films? | (do) |
| D'you like to come to see one tonight? | (would) |
| D'you like the one showing last week? | (did) |
| D'you ever seen it before? | (had) |
| Felicity's going to come tomorrow. | (is) |
| Felicity's going to come last night. | (was) |
| Felicity's gone away. | (has) |

The spelling is an attempt to reflect phonological realities rather than traditional conventions.

The identification of words and phrases can be difficult even for native speakers.[6] In English, there is a tendency in rapid speech for syllables to be left "open" and their final consonants to be attached to the beginning of the next syllable. The result is that phrases such as *not at all* or *time zone* may be misheard as *not a tall* or *time's own*. The reduction of unstressed vowels may further increase phonetic ambiguities. The central portions of the following two sentences might, for example, be pronounced indistinguishably:

I asked the way to the station.

I asked the waiter the time.[7]

Foreign learners could clearly benefit from training in recognising and interpreting the phonetic conflations that are liable to occur in the normal flow of speech. Even if the learner wants to keep syllables and words distinct in his own pronunciation, he needs to understand native speakers when they fail to do so. Dictation seems an ideal exercise for concentrating attention on this aspect of comprehension.

The problem of identifying intonation patterns might be tackled by getting the student to punctuate pairs such as:

That's your pencil?

That's my pencil.

or to underline syllables that receive the tonic.

## 16 Phrase boundaries — An exercise

In the preceding section there were a few examples of syllables and words that might become blurred in speech. There are other cases however where phrase patterns are likely to be heavily marked as these have a vital part to play in the structuring and interpretation of the sentence. The use of hyphens in the two sentences below is a visual indication of how the words are to be grouped. In speech, rhythm and intonation might convey similar information:

Old Macdonald's got twenty five-year-old sheep.

Old Macdonald's got twenty-five year-old sheep.

The foreign learner must be trained to note the significance of contrastive uses of rhythm and intonation. The following short exercise takes up the problem of grouping words into phrases and practises their identification in a simple form. The student has to write down a series of sums that he hears. The brackets indicate how the operations are to be grouped orally, and how the student should record them.

Write down the sums that you will hear me speak.

1. $2 + 2$
2. $2 + 2 + 4$
3. $(2 + 2) \times 4$
4. $(2 + 4) \times 2$
5. $2 + (4 \times 2)$
6. $(8 - 3) + 1$
7. $8 - (4 + 3)^8$

If the student had to solve these aural sums instead of recording them, he would be performing an exercise in following instructions. Before I turn to this final type of exercise, I would like to outline an advanced dictation exercise for the student of literature.

## 17 Rhythmical patterns — An exercise

The student would be asked to write down the following autobiographical passage:

"So here I am, in the middle way, having had twenty years — twenty years largely wasted . . . trying to learn to use words, and every attempt is a wholly new start and a different kind of failure because one has only learnt to get the better of words for the thing one no longer has to say, or the way in which one is no longer disposed to say it. And so each venture is a new beginning, a raid on the inarticulate with shabby equipment always deteriorating in the general mess of imprecision of feeling, undisciplined squads of emotion. And what there is to conquer, by strength or submission, has already been discovered once or twice, or several times, by men whom one cannot hope to emulate – but there is no competition – there is only the fight to recover what has been lost and found and lost again and again: and now, under conditions that seem unpropitious. But perhaps neither gain nor loss. For us, there is only the trying. The rest is not our business."

It may dawn on the student, while he is busy copying this down, that what he is listening to is not prose but poetry. The passage comes from T. S. Eliot's *Four Quartets*.

The next step is for the student to decide where the line-endings occur in the original poem. He must, in other words, determine its metre. Here is a suggested version for one part of the passage, based on Robert Speaight's recording of it:

| | |
|---|---|
| Be/cause one has/ only /learnt | 3 |
| To/get the /better of /words | 3 |
| For the /thing one no/longer /has to/say | 4 |
| Or the /way in/which one /is | 3 |
| No /longer dis/posed to/say it. | 3 |
| And /so /each /venture | 3 |
| ∧ Is a /new be/ginning . . . | 3 |

The diagonal lines indicate the beginning of each foot in a line (i.e. the occurrence of each stressed syllable) and the caret symbol '∧' in the last line indicates a silent stress or beat.[9] This is not, of course, the way in which Eliot himself recorded the lines. He wrote:

Because one has only learnt to get the better of words
For the thing one no longer has to say, or the way in which
One is no longer disposed to say it. And so each venture
Is a new beginning, a raid on the inarticulate . . .

Allowing one silent beat in the penultimate line, and two in the last, the lines can be read as hexameters, containing six feet each.

The student can be trained to hear that so-called free verse such as Eliot's has a definite rhythmical shape. But whether this is realised in three feet lines or in six feet lines, and which words are stressed (thus occasionally shifting line endings), is a matter that depends entirely on a particular reading of the poem, on a particular vocal interpretation of it. The written lines are no sure guide – Eliot himself does not always respect them in his own reading of his poems.

A dictation exercise of this kind, involving the student in recording different readings of a poem, would be a practical introduction to the phonological structuring of poetry and would raise a number of further issues about its interpretation.

## 18  Following Instructions

The texts used in previous exercises have been argumentative, descriptive, narrative, conversational, and poetic. The sums dictated to the student in one exercise were also instructional. They told him to do something. There are other forms of instructions that he may have to understand: the instructions on every tape, for instance, or those given in a recipe, a knitting pattern, a do-it-yourself kit, a magistrate's court, an examination.

The next and last exercise in this chapter begins by getting the student to follow a particular kind of instruction.

## 19  The Armchair Detective — An exercise

*Listen. The local vicar, Mr. Wagtail, has been murdered at his house. You are the police officer in charge of the investigations. The first thing every good police officer does is to make a map of the scene of the crime to establish the whereabouts of all people concerned. Get out your notebook, listen to what your sergeant tells you, and make a map.*

*Sergeant:* "Well, sir, I heard the shot at 10 pm. and immediately proceeded to the front door. The lodger, Mr. McHeath, let me in. As you go in, there's this big room on your left running the whole length of the house. It's the sitting room, and that's where the body was. Immediately opposite, across the passage, is the dining room. That's where Mr. McHeath said he was until he heard the shot. Then there's the kitchen beyond the dining room, and at the end of the passage the stairs. When you get upstairs you've got the bathroom on your right, and that's where Mr. Bream, the curate, was. He was making a proper din, banging to be let out. Then next to the bathroom is the Wagtails' bedroom and on the other side of the passage the children's room which Miss Tattle was using as a study. The only other room is the guest room opposite the bathroom . . . What? oh yes, all the rooms have got only one door on to the passage, except the Wagtails' bedroom which has got a connecting door to the bathroom. . . ."

*Have you finished your plan, writing down all the names of the rooms and who was in them? But we don't know where one person was. Who is it? . . . Yes, Mrs. Wagtail. The sergeant talked about the Wagtails' bedroom and their children's bedroom, so there must be a Mrs. Wagtail. The children were away, but where was she?*

*Sergeant:* "Who, Mrs. Wagtail? In the kitchen of course."

*Now check your plan with the sergeant's own. You'll find it on page 2 of your notebook:*

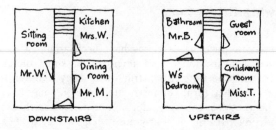

The next step in the exercise would be to get the student to establish the means, motives, and opportunity of each of the suspects in the case from the statements they make and the observations of the sergeant. From here he could be led on to draw conclusions about who could have, or must have, committed the crime and why. The student could finish the exercise by writing a report on his findings or by drawing up a case for the prosecution.

Making inferences and expressing conclusions is a particularly important aspect of language behaviour to practise. Many higher secondary school pupils, for example, find it difficult to do this in a foreign language.[10] Their written work, at least, suffers from a poverty of logical connectives and hence displays little logical structure. Exercises on the lines indicated above not only helped them to write more coherently, they also effected an over-all improvement in style and correctness. It seems that once a student can co-ordinate his ideas clearly, he is less inclined to commit minor structural errors or to translate literally from his mother tongue. But here we are trespassing on the territory of the next chapter. Following instructions and listening to evidence are clearly comprehension exercises. Expressing conclusions and learning to structure one's own ideas are more properly the objects of production exercises.

NOTES

1. The use of multiple-choice to test reading comprehension is excellently illustrated in the S.R.A. Reading Laboratory. Any teacher wishing for ideas on the choice of aural comprehension texts, and the design of questions, should study these materials.
2. These examples are taken from P. Roberts: *Understanding English*, Harper & Brothers, New York, 1958.
3. Mary Webb: *Precious Bane*.
4. The symbols and abbreviations used in the following exercises are based on those recommended by J-F. Rozan: *La Prise de Notes en Interprétation Consécutive* Ecole des Interprètes, Geneva 1965.
   They include the use of abbreviated or shorter words (eg. tho, but); and of note-taking symbols which indicate a general idea or direction, their precise meaning being determined by the context. The symbols are:

→ movement forward to another point eg. leads to, results in, arrives

← movement from a point eg. comes from, receives, suffers from

↗ development or success eg. progresses, improves

↙ decline or failure eg. regresses, decreases

= equals sign eg. like, corresponding to, the same as

≠ difference sign eg. not the same as, is not comparable

− underlining for emphasis eg. very

=double underlining for increased emphasis eg. most

=double broken underlining for attenuation eg. very little

? a question, problem

5. In most Scots and in some English dialects the last pair are phonemically contrasted rather than homophonous.
6. R. J. Wales, and J. C. Marshall "The organization of linguistic performance" in *Psycholinguistics Papers* ed. J. Lyons and R. J. Wales.
7. *Psycholinguistics Papers,* Morton, op. cit.
8. This exercise was designed by Gordon Taylor.
9. For the source of these techniques of metrical notation, see D. Abercrombie: "A Phonetician's View of Verse Structure," in *Studies in Phonetics and Linguistics,* Oxford University Press, 1965, and "Syllable Quantity and Enclitics in English" in *In Honour of Daniel Jones,* Longman, 1964.
10. Deborah Mansergh: "Dissertation for the Diploma in Applied Linguistics", Edinburgh, 1966. These findings are based on Miss Mansergh's own research and on her study of British "A" Level Examiners' Reports.

# 7 Production exercises

*Sie ist nämlich die sich ewig wiederholende Arbeit des Geistes, den artikulierten Laut zum Ausdruck des Gedanken fähig zu machen.*

*Sie muss daher von endlichen Mitteln einen unendlichen Gebrauch machen.*[1]

— VON HUMBOLDT

## 1 Drills, problems and production exercises

Wilhelm von Humboldt, who is quoted above, characterises speech as a creation process (*eine Erzeugung*) rather than a dead, created work (*ein todtes Erzeugtes*). If we teach English exclusively as a text book language (i.e. as written and spoken prose), that can be drilled to the limits of its structures, we may risk killing it both as an object of interest and as a means to communication in the mind of the learner. Exercises attempt to bring it to life there. Comprehension exercises show it to be a living thing outside him, problems try to recreate it inside him, and production exercises encourage him to develop his own creativity. Drills may make us think of a language as something finite, a list of structures, that can automatically be imprinted on the learner by a sufficiency of prompts and responses. Von Humboldt reminds us that language is unlimited, and that it has to be invented afresh by each learner and user. We can give him examples and suggest rules, but it is the learner who has to internalise these as operational realities. Problems are designed to help him perceive the rules underlying the examples. Production exercises encourage him to apply the rules in the invention of his own utterances.

## 2 Types of production exercises

The purpose of a production exercise is to extract a continuous or evolving linguistic response from the learner. It might take the form of a rhyme or a poem, a passage of spoken prose, or a part in a conversation. His activities may be assigned to one or other of six types:

1. Repetition.
2. Reading aloud.
3. Translation.
4. Answering questions.
5. Role-playing.
6. Playing a game.

There is a gradation in the difficulty of these types of exercise, so we shall consider them one at a time.

## 3 Repetition exercises

Repetition is a re-creative and recreational exercise rather than a creative one. When it proceeds to the extent of learning things by heart, it has its place in language learning. Many foreign language learners certainly believe in learning things by heart, particularly important things like irregular verbs and examination answers.

Leaving these aside, the things that can be most profitably repeated and rehearsed in the language laboratory are rhymes, conversations and, of course, the right answers to any questions or cues we set in other kinds of drill and exercise.

Learning rhymes and conversations can provide the learner with an anchorage in the language, familiar territory in which he makes no mistakes and knows what is coming next. From this home ground, he can be encouraged to make a number of forays into the language. For instance, I introduced my Indian primary school pupils to the present tense through the song:

This is the way I get out of bed

(wash my face, go to school etc.)

At seven o'clock in the morning.

Once they learnt the song, it was easy to ask them, and they already knew how to answer from the words of the song itself, when they really did get out of bed, go to school, do their sums, eat their dinner etc.

But of course I had to make sure that they understood what they were repeating and repeated it correctly. The onus is all on the teacher, for a failure on either count in no way detracts from their pleasure in reciting. One of my pupils, for example, with a fine ear for alliteration and rhyme, vigorously sang:

This is the why I wash my face. . . .

He was following the strategy of converting the unfamiliar coinage into the familiar — the word *way* was unknown to him. This strategy is one of which we must be beware, whether our pupils are reading or reciting. For learners, too, have "ears like errant wings".[2]

Through repetition exercises we can introduce and rehearse all aspects of language from sound structures to the minutest changes in tone of voice indicating attitudes and feelings. A. A. Milne's poem, "The King's Breakfast", is a perfect occasion for the latter. It suggests everything to the listener from the sleepy irony of the cow, through the gullibility of the maid, the superiority of the queen, the reassuringness of all three to the king's peevish protests, down to his delighted responses, and his final cautious reminder:

"But I do like a little bit of butter for my bread."[3]

This rhyme also practises every sound in the English language, the preservation of a regular rhythm, the intonation for questions and answers, the formation of polite requests (*"Could we have some butter for the royal slice of bread?"*) and negative commands (*"Don't forget the butter..."*), the contrast between *like* and *would like* (*"Would you like to try a little marmalade instead?"*, *"I do like a little bit...."*), and finally the contrast between statements in the past tense (narrative) and in the present (conversation).

Repetition, then, can serve as a means of familiarisation and rehearsal. But rehearsing and acting are not the same as taking part in a real conversation. Something may be said to the learner which the familiar exercises have not prepared him to understand. Or he may want to say something which he has not had the chance of practising before.

## 4   Reading aloud exercises

Reading aloud into a tape-recorder is the reverse process of dictation. It can therefore train the learner to differentiate *orally* between the sounds and phrases he has to distinguish *aurally* in Chapter 6 (section 14), and to differentiate in his pronunciation between homographs, words that are spelt in the same way but spoken differently. Reading aloud could also give practice, if this was thought desirable, in the techniques of assimilation and elision indicated in the same earlier chapter, and in Chapter 4 (section 6). It could also get the learner to convey his attitude through variations in his tone of voice. He could be asked to read the same sentence aloud in such a way that it conveys an unspoken message to the hearer:

Won't you stay for dinner?    (*Please do!*)

Won't you stay for dinner?    (*It's time you went!*)

Finally, reading aloud could be used to teach the pronunciation of two different kinds of words: foreign words that English people say in a funny way; English words that foreign people say in a funny way. The first is illustrated by the pronunciation of *data* and *a priori* in Chapter 6(section 7), the second by the pronunciation, in the speech of some foreigners, of the names of such domestically unsung heroes as Mr. Oneshoe Chee Chee, and Lord Carjohn.[4]

Reading aloud has perhaps become unfashionable in modern language teaching. Some teachers feel that it places emphasis on the written language rather than on the spoken, and that a too early introduction to English spelling may actually hinder the acquisition of a good accent if the learner comes to trust his eyes more than his ears. It is certainly true that reading aloud effectively or intelligibly is a rather specialised skill which even many native speakers may not have mastered. But it would be a pity to reject it altogether as a training exercise for these reasons. Given due aural preparation, reading aloud may help the learner to remember what he has heard. Visual and aural image combine to reinforce each other. And the language laboratory is an ideal place in which to practise. The rest of the class are not confined to following the text while one of them reads. They can all read at the same time in the laboratory. And if a model version has been recorded on the tape, they can check their pronunciation against this, and repeat sections with which they or the teacher are not satisfied.

## 5 Translation exercises

Translation has also become unfashionable except in training schools for interpreters. Like reading aloud, rapid or sensitive translation is a specialised skill. Many people who can speak two languages fluently are clumsy or slow at translating from one to the other.

Translation exercises are not advocated here as a way of learning to talk. Clearly we would like our pupils to listen to and speak the new language as early as possible without constant recourse to translation. But translation exercises may serve in a limited role as a means of drawing the learner's attention to points of divergence between his mother tongue and the language he is learning. Some of these relate to what is said in particular situations, to linguistic good manners. Such points can probably be adequately coped with in the role-playing exercises of the next section. Other divergences concern grammatical and lexical usage. These could form a proper subject for occasional translation exercises.

Divergences in grammar and vocabulary may take two forms. First, there is the problem of cognate terms. Two languages may possess vocabulary items or grammatical structures which are superficially similar but in fact differ in the roles they play. This may cause learners to use a term or structure inappropriately on an analogy with how it is employed in their mother tongue. Secondly, there are the problems created when one language makes a distinction which is not observed in the other. Here learners of the first language may fail to make the distinction at all, or may misapprehend its nature.

The problem of cognate terms can be illustrated by comparing French and Bengali with English. All three languages possess a perfect tense form distinct from the simple past. Very often verbs in the perfect tense of one language can be translated into the same tense in the other. But not always. An Englishman would use the perfect tense if he wanted to indicate the duration of a process:

I have been waiting for a long time.

The Frenchman would, in these circumstances, use his present tense:

J' attends depuis longtemps.

Similarly an Englishman might use the perfect tense to convey the immediacy of an action:

I have just passed my exam.

But a Bengali might prefer his past tense for this situation:

ami ekhoni egjamin pash korlam.

On the vocabulary level, both Frenchmen and Englishmen talk about *smoking*, but the Frenchman uses the word to refer to a dinner jacket. Bengalis and Englishmen both use the word *panting*, but in Bengali it is applied to trouser material.

The second kind of divergence, in which a single term in one language corresponds to two or more in another, can be illustrated through a comparison of Spanish and Bengali with English. English only has one verb *to be*. Spanish has two, *ser* and *estar*, which occur in different environments.

Soy profesor. (I am a teacher.)

Estoy en Calcuta. (I am in Calcutta.)

or contrastively in the same environment:

Soy gordo. (I am fat by nature.)

Estoy gordo. (I am fat at the moment.)

Bengali has four ways of expressing *to be:* where we would use this verb to describe states, no verb is permitted at all. Locative, processive and existential statements, on the other hand, each require a separate verb:

Ami kushi. (I am happy.)

ami Kolkatae thaki. (I am in Calcutta.)

brishti hochhe. (Rain is = it is raining.)

cha achhe. (Tea is = there is some tea.)

The words *teacher* and *professor* involve a vocabulary divergence between English and Spanish. The Spanish professor is called a *catedratico*, while any kind of teacher is a *profesor* down to the rural primary school master, or *maestro*. Spanish thus has one more term than English to describe teachers. Bengali, in contrast, uses the single verb *khaoa* to describe the processes of eating, drinking, and smoking.

There may be asymmetries of hyponymic structure in the languages as well as of application. The Spanish *profesor* covers all grades of teacher down to a maestro, but there is no cover term for the exclusive use of university teachers who, in England, might all be called lecturers (or dons in Oxford and Cambridge). Similarly there is no superordinate term in Bengali which includes green peppers as well as other vegetables, but nuts are regarded as a kind of *phol* (fruit).

## 6 Role-playing exercises

Role-playing requires more from the student than repetition or reading aloud. He has to assume a role in a conversation and to contribute to it accordingly. Which roles and which situations it is worth rehearsing will depend on why the student is learning the language. Tourists may want to practise asking directions, booking accommodation, making travel arrangements etc. Businessmen and airline pilots will be interested in situations that arise in the course of their professions.

Whatever the role undertaken, the learner's side of the conversation can be prompted in the laboratory. Cue-words can be given in his mother tongue or in the second language. Pictures and sound-effects can be employed. Occasionally the context itself will be sufficient to indicate a probable response. Model versions of the conversation can be recorded on the tape for the student to consult. But the object of the exercise is to get the student to invent what he has to say as the conversation develops. The fairly elementary exercise that follows illustrates the use of picture prompts.

## 7 Shopping — An exercise

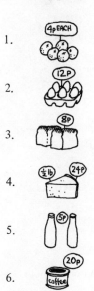

*Taped instructions and answers*

1.

*Ex. 1.* **Look at picture 1.**
How many oranges are there?

_____

2.

**Look at picture 2.**
How many eggs are there?

_____

3.

**Look at picture 3.**
How many loaves of bread are there?

_____

4.

**Look at picture 4.**
How much cheese is there?

_____

5.

**Look at picture 5.**
How many bottles of milk are there?

_____

6.

**Look at picture 6.**
How many tins of coffee are there?

_____

*Ex. 2.* How much does one orange cost?

How much do the eggs cost?

How much does one loaf of bread cost?

How much does half a pound of cheese cost?

How much does a bottle of milk cost?

How much does the tin of coffee cost?

| | |
|---|---|
| *Ex. 3.* | **Now play the part of a customer.** **Look at picture 1. Listen.** |
| **Voice:** | Good morning. Can I help you? |
| **Student:** | *I'd like 5 oranges. How much is that?* |
| | **Look at picture 2.** |
| **Voice:** | Good morning, can I help you? |
| **Student:** | *I'd like half a dozen eggs. How much is that?* |
| | **Look at picture 3.** |
| **Voice:** | Good morning. Can I help you? |
| **Student:** | *I'd like two loaves of bread. How much is that?* |
| | **Look at picture 4 etc.** |
| | |
| *Ex. 4.* | **Now play the part of the shopkeeper.** **Look at picture 1. (ping!)** |
| **Student:** | *Good morning. Can I help you?* |
| **Voice:** | I'd like 5 oranges. How much is that? |
| **Student:** | *That'll be 20p.* |
| | **Look at picture 2. (ping!)** |
| **Student:** | *Good morning, can I help you?* |
| **Voice:** | I'd like half a dozen eggs. How much is that? |
| **Student:** | *That'll be 12p.* |
| | **Look at picture 3. (ping!)** |
| **Student:** | *Good morning, can I help you?* |
| **Voice:** | I'd like two loaves of bread. How much is that? |
| **Student:** | *That'll be 16p.* |
| | **Look at picture 4 etc.** |

| | |
|---|---|
| *Ex. 5.* | **Now play the part of the customer again. Look at pictures 1 and 2.** |
| Voice: | Can I help you? |
| Student: | *I'd like five oranges, please.* |
| Voice: | Anything else? |
| Student: | *Yes, I also want half a dozen eggs. How much is that?* |
| | **Look at pictures 3 and 4.** |
| Voice: | Can I help you? |
| Student: | *I'd like two loaves of bread, please.* |
| Voice: | Anything else? |
| Student: | *Yes, I also want half a pound of cheese. How much is that?* |
| | **Look at pictures 5 and 6.** |
| Voice: | Can I help you? |
| Student: | *I'd like two bottles of milk, please.* |
| Voice: | Anything else? |
| Student: | *Yes, I also want a tin of coffee. How much is that?* |
| Voice: | Do you want a big tin or a small tin? |
| Student: | *A small tin.* |
| *Ex. 6.* | **Now play the part of the shopkeeper. (ping!)** |
| Student: | *Can I help you?* |
| Voice: | I'd like five oranges, please. |
| Student: | *Anything else?* |
| Voice: | Yes, I also want half a dozen eggs. How much is that? |
| Student: | *That'll be 32p altogether.* |
| | **Now look at pictures 3 and 4. (ping!)** |
| Student: | *Can I help you?* |
| Voice: | I'd like two loaves of bread, please. |
| Student: | *Anything else?* |

| | |
|---|---|
| **Voice:** | Yes, I also want half a pound of cheese. |
| | How much is that? |
| **Student:** | *That'll be 40p altogether.* |
| | **Now look at pictures 5 and 6. (ping!)** |
| **Student:** | *Can I help you?* |
| **Voice:** | I'd like two bottles of milk, please. |
| **Student:** | *Anything else?* |
| **Voice:** | Yes, I also want a small tin of coffee. |
| | How much is that? |
| **Student:** | *That'll be 30p altogether.* |
| **Voice:** | Here you are. 30p exactly. |
| **Student:** | *Thank you. Good morning.* |

## 8   Analysis of the exercise in shopping

The language prompted in these exercises is fairly limited. *I would like* and *I want* are both suggested as ways of asking for something. A small sample of countable and uncountable nouns are constantly employed. The student is given a little practice in mental arithmetic and in using conversational phrases such as *good morning, please* and *thank you.* The pictures and the voice of the other speaker give the only clues as to what he is to say next, though he can consult the suggested answers on the tape if he is in doubt. Occasionally the strange voice breaks the pattern of the exercise to check that the student is not responding too mechanically.

Obviously more varied and more ambitious role-playing exercises could be designed employing any or all of the types of prompt suggested in Section 6 of this chapter. But, as in repetition exercises, there is ultimately a limit to what can be anticipated and adequately rehearsed. Role-playing exercises can introduce the student to stock situations and to some of the stock responses in them. They help to make him more independent in the language, trusting in his appraisal of the situation and in his appreciation of the significance of the small cues to an expected response that may be given in real conversations. But sooner or later he will find that he cannot forever be playing predictable roles. He will have to learn to be himself and to speak for himself.

## 9   Question-answering exercises

Question-answering exercises can take the student one step further towards self-expression. In the previous chapter, questions were used to test his comprehension. But they can also elicit personal information from a student. In the next exercise, this procedure is preceded by a long series of prompts which build up and rehearse someone else's biographical details, thus providing a model to which the student can adapt his own. For the sake of space, the successive steps of prompt, student's response, confirmation and student's repetition in this linear programme have been condensed into a single running format. The longer responses would be broken up into single sentences in the laboratory. The student has the prompts in a booklet before him. He records his responses, and he hears the right answers on the tape.

## 10 Time and place — An exercise

1. I have a friend called Rao. He is a Madrasi, but he lives
   ........ Calcutta.
   *He lives in Calcutta.*

2. But he comes ......................... Madras.
   *He lives in Calcutta but he comes from Madras.*

3. He lives ....................... a house.
   *He lives in a house.*

4. His house is ....................... Rashbehari Avenue.
   *His house is in Rashbehari Avenue.*

5. He ....................... Rashbehari Avenue.
   *He lives in Rashbehari Avenue.*

6. The number of his house is 63. So, he lives ................... 63, Rashbehari Avenue.
   *He lives at 63, Rashbehari Avenue.*

7. Notice that we say:
   (i)   He lives ....................................Calcutta.
         *He lives in Calcutta.*
   (ii)  He lives ....................................a house.
         *He lives in a house.*
   (iii) He lives...............................................Rashbehari Avenue.
         *He lives in Rashbehari Avenue.*
   (iv)  He lives ..............................................63, Rashbehari Avenue.
         *He lives at 63, Rashbehari Avenue.*

8. We talk about living ........................ a town, or a street, or a building, but living ....................... an address.
   This is the rule: **We live *in* a town, or a building or a street, but we live *at* an address.**

9. So, my friend ....................... Calcutta, but he ....................... Madras.
   He ....................... 63, Rashbehari Avenue.
   *My friend lives in Calcutta, but he comes from Madras. He lives at 63, Rashbehari Avenue.*

10. He is a bank clerk. He works ........................ a bank.
    *He works in a bank.* (We could also say, he works at a bank, but let's use *in*).

11. So, he works ........................ bank.
    *He works in a bank.*

12. Don't forget to use the indefinite article *a* here.
    (i) He lives.............. house.    *He lives in a house.*
    (ii) He works............. bank.    *He works in a bank.*

13. His house is two miles ........................ bank.
    *His house is two miles from the bank.*
    Notice that this time you must use the definite article *the*. We have already mentioned that he works in a bank, and the next time we mention the bank, we must use the definite article.

14. So, my friend lives................................... but he...................
    .................................. He.................................................... 63,
    .............................. He ................................................ bank. His
    house.................................................... bank.
    *My friend lives in Calcutta but he comes from Madras. He lives at 63, Rashbehari Avenue. He works in a bank. His house is two miles from the bank.*

15. He has to ............................................................... bed at 6 a.m.
    *He has to get out of bed at 6 a.m.*
    We can also say: he has to get up.
    Let's use the shorter phrase and say:

16. He gets.................... 6 a.m.
    *He gets up at 6 a.m.*

17. He gets up at 6 o'clock ........................... morning.
    *He gets up at 6 o'clock in the morning.*
    Don't forget to use the definite article with *morning*.

18. So, he gets up at 6 o'clock in the morning. He has to start work at 9 o'clock. His house is two miles ........................... bank, so he has to .............................. home at 8.15.
    *His house is two miles from the bank, so he has to leave home at 8.15.*
    We can also say: he leaves his house at 8.15. But let's use the word *home*.

19. So, he ............................... at 6 o'clock ................................ morning.
    He ............................... 8.15 to go ............................. bank.
    *He gets up at 6 o'clock in the morning. He leaves home at 8.15 to go to the bank.*

20. He takes a tram to the bank.
    He goes............................... bank................................. tram.
    *He goes to the bank by tram.*

21. Can you remember which prepositions we use after different verbs?
    (i) He lives .............................Calcutta.
    > *He lives in Calcutta.*

    (ii) He lives ..................................a house.
    > *He lives in a house.*

    (iii) He lives ...............................................63, Rashbehari Avenue.
    > *He lives at 63, Rashbehari Avenue.*

    (iv) He works .......................................a bank.
    > *He works in a bank.*

    (v) He goes .................................the bank.
    > *He goes to the bank.*

22. So, my friend.................................................... 8.15. He.......................
    ............bank...........................tram. He............................. to the
    bank at 9 o'clock.
    > *He leaves home at 8.15. He goes to the bank by tram. He gets to the bank at 9 o'clock.*

23. Could we also say: *He goes to the bank at 9 o'clock?* Yes or no?

    > *No*, this would mean the same as he leaves home at 9 o'clock.

24. But we know that he leaves home at ..........................
    > *He leaves home at 8.15.*

25. What we want to say is something that means the same as he reaches the bank at 9 o'clock. So we must say:
    He.......................... to the bank at 9 o'clock.
    > *He gets to the bank at 9 o'clock.*

26. Banks like their employees to be on time. So he never
    .......... to the bank ..........................
    > *He never gets to the bank late.*

27. He is .......................... the bank all day long.
    > *He is at* (or *in*) *the bank all day long.*

28. He is at the bank....................... 9 a.m. ................................. 5 p.m.
    > *He is at the bank from 9 a.m. until 5 p.m.*
    > (We could also say from 9 a.m. to 5 p.m., up till 5 p.m., or till 5 p.m. But let's use *until.*)

29. He is............................. bank............................ 9 o'clock....................
    morning ................................5 o'clock ...................................
    .......................... afternoon.
    > *He is at the bank from 9 o'clock in the morning until 5 o'clock in the afternoon.*

30. But he doesn't have much work to do after 3 o'clock and he usually finishes his work at or before 4.30. He usually finishes his work ........... 4.30. (See if you can use only one preposition which means the same as *at or before.*)
    *He usually finishes his work by 4.30.*

31. Here *by* means the same as *at or before.*
    So, my friend usually finishes his work ..................... 4.30, but he has to stay ...................... bank ....................... 5 o'clock.
    *He finishes his work by 4.30 but he has to stay at the bank until 5 o'clock.*

32. At 5 o'clock he ...................... the bank.
    *At 5 o'clock he leaves the bank.*

33. Can you remember which verbs are followed by which prepositions?
    (i) He goes ..................... the bank.
    *He goes to the bank.*
    (ii) He gets ..................... the bank.
    *He gets to the bank.*
    (iii) He is ....................... the bank.
    *He is at the bank.*
    (iv) He stays ................... the bank.
    *He stays at the bank.*
    (v) He leaves ................. the bank.
    *He leaves the bank.*

34. The verb *leave* doesn't take any preposition here. *Go* and *get* are both followed by *to*. *Be* and *stay* are followed by *at* (or *in*).
    So, my friend ....................... bank at 5 o'clock. At 5 o'clock he ..................... home.
    *At 5 o'clock he goes* (or *returns,* or *comes*) *home.*

35. It is unnecessary to say: *He goes back home* (or *he comes back home*). If my friend leaves his spectacles in the bank, he will go ...................
    ......... to the bank to fetch them.
    *He will go back to the bank.*

36. Here we have to use the word *back* to show that he is returning to the bank. But when we speak of *going home* or *coming home* these phrases by themselves carry the meaning of *returning.* We don't need to use the word *back.*
    So my friend leaves ............................................. 5 o'clock.
    He goes ............................................. at 5 o'clock.
    *He leaves the bank at 5 o'clock. He goes home at 5 o'clock.*

37. He ..................................... home at 5.45.
    *He gets* (or *comes,* or *reaches,* or *arrives* or *returns*) *home at 5.45.*

38. Have you noticed when we have to use prepositions and articles and when we don't use them?
    (i) He goes................. bank.    *He goes to the bank.*
    (ii) He comes............. bank.    *He comes to the bank.*
    (iii) He gets................ bank.    *He gets to the bank.*
    (iv) He goes...............home.    *He goes home.*
    (v) He comes............ home.    *He comes home.*
    (vi) He gets...............home.    *He gets home.*

39. After verbs like *go, come* and *get* we do not use any preposition before the word *home,* and the word *home* is not preceded by any article.
Would it ever be possible to say: *He is going to the home?* Yes or no?
*Yes.* We can say *he is going to the home* but it means something very different. It would mean that he was going to an institution such as a Children's Home. We could also say *he is going to the home of a friend.* In either case, *the home* is somebody else's home (or Home). It's not his own home.
Let's get back to my friend.

40. So, my friend gets.....................bank at 9 o'clock. He is.....................
.............bank.................9..............................morning............................
5.....................................................afternoon. He usually finishes his work
.....................4.30, but he has to.............................bank............................
5. At 5 he .....................................................................home. He..........home at 5.45.
*My friend gets to the bank at 9 o'clock. He is at the bank from 9 in the morning until 5 in the afternoon. He usually finishes his work by 4.30, but he has to stay at the bank until 5. At 5, he goes home. He gets home at 5.45.*

41. Then he .............................a short rest.
*He has a short rest.*

42. Then he ......................... bath.
*He has a bath* (or *his bath*).

43. He ......................... evening meal at 9.30.
*He has* (or *eats*) *his evening meal at 9.30.*

44. Notice that we say:
    (i) He ......................... rest.    *He has a rest.*
    (ii) He .........................bath.    *He has a bath* (or *his bath*).
    (iii) He ......................... meal.    *He has a meal* (or *his meal*).
It would be wrong to say:
He takes bath.
He takes rest.
He takes meal.

45. So, my friend .......................... home at 5 o'clock. He ....................
at 5.45. He .............................. rest, he ....................... bath, and he
................ ........ dinner at 9.30.
*My friend goes home at 5 o'clock. He gets home at 5.45. He has a rest,*
*he has a bath and he has his dinner at 9.30.*

46. He has his dinner at 9.30 ............................. evening.
*He has his dinner at 9.30 in the evening.*

47. Then he ............................. bed.
*Then he goes to bed.*

48. Notice that we say:
    (i) He goes ................. bank.    *He goes to the bank.*
    (ii) He goes ................ home.    *He goes home.*
    (iii) He goes .................. bed.    *He goes to bed.*

49. Would it ever be possible to say: *He goes to the bed?* Yes or no?

    *Yes.* We could say *he goes to the bed,* but it would mean something
    quite different.

50. Imagine that my friend is very nervous. He is afraid that thieves may
    be hiding under his bed. So every evening he goes ..........................
    ........... bed and looks underneath it.
    *He goes to the bed* and looks underneath it to see if any thieves are
    hiding there.

51. After that he ............................. bed.
    *He goes to bed.*

52. *Go to bed* means the same as going to sleep. But *Go to the bed* means
    approaching a particular bed, without any intention necessarily of
    sleeping in it.
    So, my friend ................................... bed at or before 11.30 p.m.
    *He goes to bed.*

53. He ......................... dinner ....................... 9.30 ........................... evening
    and ........................... bed ................... 11.30 ........................... night.
    *He has his dinner at 9.30 in the evening and goes to bed by 11.30 at*
    *night.*

54. Notice that we say:
    (i) 9 o'clock ............................... morning
                            *9 o'clock in the morning.*
    (ii) 5 o'clock ............................... afternoon
                            *5 o'clock in the afternoon.*
    (iii) 9.30 ........................................ evening
                            *9.30 in the evening.*
    (iv) 11.30 ................... night.    *11.30 at night.*

55. Would it ever be possible to say:
   (i) at the morning         Yes or no? ............................ *No.*
   (ii) at the evening        Yes or no? ............................ *No.*
   (iii) at the night          Yes or no? ............................ *No.*
   (iv) in the night          Yes or no? ............................ *Yes.*
It would be wrong to say *at the morning; at the evening; at the night.* But we could say *in the night.* However, it would mean something different.

56. My friend goes to bed by 11.30 .................... night, but he often wakes up .................... night, thinking that he can hear noises coming from under his bed.
*He goes to bed at 11.30 at night but he often wakes up in the night.* Here you can see that *in the night* means the same as *during the night.*

57. So, my friend ......................... home at 5 o'clock. He .........................
............... 5.45. He ...................... rest, then he ..........................
................. He ........................................................................ at 9.30
.................................... evening. He ...............................................
........... 11.30 ............................................................. Sometimes he wakes up ........................................................... When he finally goes to sleep, he sleeps ~.......................................... 6 o'clock the next morning.
*My friend goes home at 5 o'clock. He gets home at 5.45. He has a rest, then he has a bath. He has his dinner at 9.30 in the evening. He goes to bed by 11.30 at night. Sometimes he wakes up in the night. He sleeps until 6 o'clock the next morning.*

58. He ......................... home early ..................... Saturday afternoons.
*He comes (or goes, or gets, or returns) home early on Saturday afternoons.*

59. He doesn't ......................... bank ......................... Sundays.
*He doesn't go to the bank on Sundays.*

60. Have you noticed which prepositions are used with different kinds of time expression?
   (i) He starts work ............................................ 9 o'clock.
          *He starts work at 9 o'clock.*
   (ii) He works ................................................ morning.
          *He works in the morning.*
   (iii) He works ................................................ Saturday mornings.
          *He works on Saturday mornings.*
   (iv) He works ................................................ Mondays.
          *He works on Mondays.*
   (v) He doesn't work ............................... night.
          *He doesn't work at night.*

134 *The Language Laboratory and Language Learning*

61. We use the preposition *on* with the names of the days of the week. So, my friend doesn't work ............................................................ afternoons. ............................................................. he stays .................................. home all day.
*He doesn't work on Saturday afternoons. On Sunday(s) he stays at home all day.*

62. Notice that we say:
    (i) He goes ................... bank. *He goes to the bank.*
    (ii) He goes ............... home. *He goes home.*
    (iii) He stays ................ bank. *He stays at the bank.*
    (iv) He stays .............. home. *He stays at home.*

63. Can you remember the whole story about my friend?
My friend ............................................. Calcutta but he ...................... ................... Madras. He ................................... 63, Rashbehari Avenue. He works ................................................ His house is two miles ................................................................ He ............................ ...........................6 o'clock ........................... morning. He ................. ...................... breakfast and ............................... home at 8.15. He ...................................................tram. He................................... bank at 9 o'clock. He always................................there on time. He is ........................................... bank all............................... He often finishes his work ..................... 4.30 but he doesn't .......................... ................... bank................... 5 o'clock. He............................... home at 5 o'clock. He............. home at 5.45. Then he................................ ...............rest. Next, he ..................................... He ...................... ............................. at 9.30 ................................................ evening and ......................................... 11.30 .................................................night He doesn't work................................................................ and he stays.............................................................. Sundays.

*My friend lives in Calcutta but he comes from Madras. He lives at 63, Rashbehari Avenue. He works in (or at) a bank. His house is two miles from the bank. He gets up (or gets out of bed) at 6 o'clock in the morning. He has (not takes!) his breakfast and leaves home at 8.15. He goes to the bank by tram. He gets to (or reaches, or arrives at) the bank at 9 o'clock. He always gets there on time. He is at the bank all day (long). He often finishes his work by 4.30 but he doesn't leave the bank until (or before) 5 o'clock. He goes (or returns) home at 5 o'clock. He gets (or reaches, or arrives, or comes) home at 5.45. Then he has a short rest. Next, he has a (or his) bath. He has his dinner (or evening meal) at 9.30 in the evening and goes to bed by 11.30 at night. He doesn't work on Saturday afternoon(s) and he stays at home all day (long) on Sundays.*

Now see if you can answer the questions on the tape. Speak your answers aloud.
    (i)    Where do you come from?

    (ii)    Where do you live, (in what city or village, street and house)?
   (iii)    Where do you work or study?
   (iv)    How far is where you live from where you work or study?
    (v)    How do you get there?
   (vi)    When do you leave home in the morning?
  (vii)    When do you get up?
 (viii)    When do you get home?
   (ix)    What do you do in the evening?
    (x)    When do you go to bed?
   (xi)    What do you do on Saturday afternoons and Sundays?

Now write down on the last page of this booklet a full description of your daily routine in continuous prose. Show it to your teacher when you have finished it.

## 11   Analysis of the exercise on time and place

The structural points in the last exercise are the use of prepositions and articles with expressions of time and place set in the present tense. The semantic points are the use of this tense to express habitual actions, and the meaning contrasts between *go* and *get, at night* and *in the night, home* and *the home* etc. The student's attention is also drawn to stylistic variations and grammatical impossibilities, in the latter case making a use of negative examples which will assume more prominence in the problems of the next chapter. The negative examples are all instances of mistakes actually made in similar contexts by the adult Bengali students for whom the programme was designed, and which they might therefore be tempted to repeat in the course of the exercise. The open-ended questions at the end are, in one sense, the object of the whole exercise. But any further mistakes made in the process of answering them can only be sporadically checked by the teacher until they are recorded in writing.

It might be asked: What is the point of the personal interview techniques in the laboratory if nobody is listening to the interviews and the student has little chance of being immediately corrected? Admittedly this is not an ideal learning situation. But it may not be a profitless one. There are times in the acquisition of any skill when the learner has to practise on his own. This may be because the teacher has other students to supervise. But it may also be part of the teacher's approach. He wants the learner to acquire control over his own performance, to rehearse what he can do well and to check or improve his own weaknesses. We are accustomed to getting students to write on their own, bringing only the finished product for assessment by the teacher. We could employ the laboratory as a means of giving them practice in speaking on their own. The finished product would then be a recorded version of the student's best efforts.

Personal questions, moreover, are things that we may well want to practise answering on our own since they are likely to be asked frequently in everyday life. The laboratory is a good place for independent practice since it allows us to listen to how other people answer similar questions. The tape cannot, of course, anticipate our own needs exactly.

In question answering exercises, the student is given free choice of what he is going to say as well as how he is going to say it. All previous types of exercise have been able to anticipate the student's responses and supply a model answer. But if what the student is going to say is known in advance, he is not communicating any new information. He is not communicating at all in fact, he is just rehearsing how to do so. Only when the student is asked a personal question to which he knows we do not know the answer, is he faced with the problems of conveying his own meaning. Question answering exercises allow free choice and hence free communication. The questions need not be directed only to biographical details. They can also train the student in oral descriptions, definitions, explanations, arguments, inferences and conclusions. The student can be asked to describe a single picture or a series of pictures. He can be asked to explain how a model works. He can be given written information, say an extract of a railway or airline timetable, and be asked to give advice about routes. He can be given a map and be asked for directions. He can be asked for definitions or for his interpretation of a poem. He can practise telling stories or jokes. He can be asked to make inferences or express conclusions, as was suggested in the Armchair Detective Exercise. In short, we can use questions to elicit every kind of linguistic activity that is relevant to the student's needs. In every case we can supply a series of examples for analysis and imitation in the laboratory. But once the questions are put, the student must accept that he is on his own and responsible for his own performance. He can ask the teacher for advice, but only his final version will be rigorously checked for errors or infelicities. Once these have been corrected, the final version could be recorded again by the student, or the teacher might record it himself for the student to learn by heart, thus giving him the chance of imitating a model delivery of his own words. As was suggested in Chapter 3, such model tapes might then be used for listening practice with other students. The student can then have the satisfaction of oral composition not just for his own benefit but for that of the rest of the class.

Exercises can thus proceed in cycles, from listening to imitation, from role-playing to question-prompted composition, from first draught to revised edition, and back to imitation again. The early stages prepare for the student to work on his own. The last stage helps to remedy any deficiencies in his unsupervised work. But it is the central stages which give the student a means, a motive and an opportunity for communicating.

## 12  Game-playing exercises

There is a large number of games that can be played in the classroom, and a few that can be performed in the laboratory. Between them they can practise a whole variety of language points from spelling and punctuation to structure and vocabulary.[5]

Games are particularly valuable as a means of practising one form of linguistic activity. In the preceding section and in the previous chapter we have investigated in some detail how a student can be trained to answer questions. But we have not yet encountered many exercises which encourage him to ask them. Games are the principal controlled means of training a learner to ask purposeful questions. Drill techniques, such as converting indirect to direct questions or transforming statements into questions, may give the learner some control over the form of questions. But the questions he produces are pointless, as the answer is already known before the question is asked, or no answer is given at all. In games the learner can use his questions to obtain information. The information may not be of much value to him, but the enjoyment of playing a game is usually sufficient to encourage the learner to persist in his enquiries. This game, a version of "I spy",

One, two, three

What can I see?

Something in this room,

Beginning with *B*

gets the learner to ask *Yes-No* questions beginning *Is it a* ........................?, *Is it the* ..................... ? *etc.* "Animal, Vegetable or Mineral" demands alternative questions: *Is it big or small?* etc.

More complex games like "Alibi" and "Coffee pot" promote the whole range of *wh-* questions, while verbal relay games, like "Rumours" or "Consequences", can elicit all forms of indirect questions.

I shall illustrate only two laboratory games here, one practising statements and the other questions. For the first purpose, the pictures in Section 7 of this chapter could be shown to the student again, and he begins:

1. I went to the market this morning and I bought five oranges.

2. I went to the market this morning and I bought five oranges and half a dozen eggs.

3. I went to the market this morning and I bought five oranges, half a dozen eggs and two loaves of bread.

4. etc.

The time expressions and tense could be varied (*I'm going to the market tomorrow, I've just been to the market, I must go to the market to buy . . .* etc). The contrast between countable and uncountable nouns could be brought out by the use of the indefinite quantifier *some*, rather than by referring to specific quantities. The list of purchases can be indefinitely extended. In every case, the student is still making statements or promises, and is required to use the intonation pattern appropriate to long sentences that list a number of items.

For the second purpose, asking questions, a modified form of the game, *"Twenty Questions"*, could be played in the laboratory[6].

## 13 Five questions — An exercise

**"I am thinking of someone. I will give you five questions to try to guess who it is.**

Look at the prompts in front of you on page 1 of your booklet and ask me a question about each of them. I will tell you the answer. When you think you know, don't bother to ask any more questions, but check your answer by looking at the picture on page 2."

|  | *Booklet page 1.* | *Taped response and answer.* |
|---|---|---|
| 1. |  ? | *Is it a man or a woman?*<br>It's a woman. |
| 2. | British: American? | *Is she British or American?*<br>She's British. |
| 3. | Filmstar: Public figure? | *Is she a filmstar or a public figure?*<br>She's a public figure. |
| 4. | 40 +: 40 − ? | *Is she over forty or under forty?*<br>She's over forty. |
| 5. | Buckingham Palace:<br>10, Downing Street? | *Does she live in Buckingham Palace or at 10, Downing Street?*<br>She lives in Buckingham Palace. |

"Well, you have probably guessed by now. To check your guess, look at the picture on page 2 of the booklet. Then ask me some more questions to find out what I'm thinking of now. This time it's a thing."

|  | *Booklet page 2.* | *Taped response and answer.* |
|---|---|---|
| 1. | Veg.: min.? | *Is it vegetable or mineral?*<br>It's a mineral. |
| 2. | ←metal:←stone? | *Is it made of metal or stone?*<br>It's made of metal. |
| 3. | ○ : □ ? | *Is it round or square?*<br>It's round. |

| 4. 1971: 1972? | *Was it made in 1971 or 1972?* |
| | It was made in 1971. |

| 5. Cu.: Ag.? | *Is it made of copper or silver?* |
| | It's made of copper. |

If you haven't guessed by now, turn over the page and you will see that you are looking at a penny.

    *Booklet page 3.*

## 14   Comments on the question-asking game

Games may be used to practise language structures or pronunciation. But games are not themselves so much a form of practice as a *bona fide* linguistic activity. When the student plays a game in the laboratory, he is in a similar situation to when he listens to a story or a poem. He is behaving in the language, in the one case productively, in the other receptively. We have thus come as far as the laboratory could be expected to take us. With listening practice on the one hand, and games on the other, we can provide the learner with meaningful, purposeful and enjoyable experience of communication in a new language.

But the "Five Questions" game suffered from a restriction imposed by the nature of the conventional tape-recorder. The student cannot easily choose which questions he wants to ask, and he cannot order the questions in his own way. To remedy this, J. Mikos has suggested an ingenious use of the Language Master, a tape-recorder adapted to read cards rather than a spool of tape.[7] The picture and word prompts in the last game, for instance, could each be printed on a separate card with a strip of tape at the foot of each card. The student can then select which cards he wants to ask questions about in which order, insert each card in the tape-recorder, ask his question, hear the correct form of the question on the tape, and get the answer. In this game, an intelligent student would not need to ask many questions.

## 15   The limitations of exercises

The purposes and possibilities of exercises have now been outlined. It remains to summarise their limitations. These can be discussed under the headings of four different types of problem:

1. The problem of selection.

2. The problem of grading.

3. The problem of feedback.

4. The problem of self-monitoring.

Each of these will now be considered in turn.

## 16  The problem of selection

It is clearly the teacher's or the course-writer's responsibility to select the kinds of language that can be presented in the laboratory and the kinds of activity that ensue. The principles of selection are simple: interest; appropriateness for the age, language level and backgrounds of the learners; relevance to their needs. But some of the most interesting or relevant language activities cannot be satisfactorily presented in the laboratory. Not all games, for instance, can be played there. It is too confined for some of the best ones, like "Felicity's Cat", "Murder", "Hangman", or "Ghosts". It is also difficult to present real conversations, discussions, and lectures. Very often, in real life, we need to see the speaker's face and expression, or the environment in which he is talking. Language laboratory interchanges, even when pictures are used, are like conversations between people with paper bags tied over their heads. They can hear all right, but all they can see is the small print and the pictures on the paper in front of their noses. This restricts the fullness of understanding and the spontaneity of the response. Exercises, accordingly, tend to practise or simulate real performance, rather than to develop it directly. Prompt and response are voices in the wilderness, paving the way for the real world to come.

## 17  The problem of grading

Grading means ordering the content of tapes and the nature of the students' responses in a sequence that will promote ease of learning. Satisfactory grading is easily defined but not so easily achieved. What principles, for instance, should direct the grading of exercises? The conventional solutions of the structural syllabus are scarcely applicable. Exercises, as we have seen, are concerned with activities rather than with structures, and there are few traditions about which activities are simpler than, or logically antecedent to, others.

It would be an error to attempt to apply structural grading rigorously to comprehension exercises. Supposedly complex structures may be just as readily understood as simple ones. And apparently simple structures may pose more problems of interpretation than unknown ones. T. S. Eliot's line:

My end is in my beginning,

is identical in (surface) structure with

My pen is in my hand,

which we all teach in about Lesson 6 to beginners who probably already "know" the meaning of the nouns in each sentence. The familiarity of the structural form, however, does not make it any easier to grasp Eliot's meaning. This assumes its full significance only in relation to the whole poem.

Even in production exercises, the relative complexity of two structures may not be relevant to the order in which we feel they should be introduced. Suppose we wanted the learner to practise asking people to do things. It would seem more natural and more profitable to teach him to say:

Would you mind opening the window?

rather than the simple imperative

Open the window!

If the first type of request proves more difficult to produce easily, this may be as much because of its length as because of its structural complexity. In any course devoted to conversational usage, it scarcely seems necessary to delay the introduction of conditional request forms until the third year of study as some structurally graded textbooks do.

With no other guides to follow, only intuition, experience and experiment can help us to grade language laboratory exercises. The effectiveness of instruction depends on our introducing the right kind of exercise to the right extent at the right time in the right sequence.

## 18   The problem of feedback

Feedback is a technical term used by communications engineers to describe the processes by which the output of a system governs the input so as to correct the output. In so far as this term can be applied to language learning, the student's output is his response to a prompt or his selection of an alternative. The input is the suggested answer provided on the tape and any further remedial material supplied in the case of a faulty response. A branching programme is the closest we have come to a genuine feedback system. Here the student's responses determine what he is to practise next and so control the path his future responses are to take. But the entries to a branching programme exclude an important kind of activity. To obtain further input the student has only to choose from among a set of pre-arranged alternatives. He does not create his own responses or alternatives.

Yet the directing of creative language behaviour was the central task we assigned to exercises. When this objective is fulfilled, in the answering of open-ended comprehension or personal questions, the student no longer gets any immediate feedback. His output, so to speak, is left to run on under its own impetus until the end of the exercise. I suggested that suitable preparation and revision may reduce the dangers of serious mislearning or misproduction in unsupervised practice. But a danger still exists, if only because the input may not be the same as the "intake".[8] The student may fail to see the point of the examples we give, the suggested answers we provide, or the remedial exercises that follow his choice of the wrong alternative. Unlike a feedback machine, our student has to learn. A machine is already programmed to produce one kind of output and to react to another kind of input. The student, on the other hand, has to learn how to respond in the new language and he has to learn what variations in the input signify. Both processes are liable to error.

The "problems" of the next chapter are designed to reduce the gaps between input and intake. The effectiveness of the feedback process as a whole, however, ultimately depends on how far the student can master the problem of self-monitoring discussed in the next section. The final aim of instruction must be for him to perfect his own feedback system, to be capable of performing and continuing to learn on his own. But until he does so, we should note that exercises are no more certain to reduce or eliminate errors than the drills illustrated in previous chapters.

## 19  The problem of self-monitoring

*Self-monitoring* is a term devised by Marty to describe the process of checking and correcting one's own responses against the model versions provided on the tape. Marty noticed that many American College students failed to detect discrepancies between their own pronunciation and the recorded models.[9] Such failures are scarcely surprising in the early stages when a learner's ear may be just as unpractised as his tongue. Breakdowns in self-monitoring are less common in structural drills, though the student may occasionally ignore a difference in word-endings or wrongly interpret a weak form.

That such breakdowns can occur, however, suggests the need for several precautionary measures:

1. **Aural discrimination practice:** The learner's ears can be trained to discriminate between sounds, words, and features of intonation from an early stage. Such practice can take the form of a game, inside or outside the laboratory, and can be enjoyed by children as well as by adults. Several examples of discrimination drills have appeared in earlier chapters. It should also be remembered that extensive listening practice may by itself encourage and develop aural discrimination. Some learners may fail to use their ears properly simply because they have not had enough opportunity of doing so.

2. **The presence of a teacher:** Extensive listening and discrimination practice help the learner to distinguish between sounds etc. in the foreign language. They may not succeed, however, in teaching him to distinguish between his own ways of producing such sounds and a native-speaker's. Many learners display excellent understanding but poor reproduction. In

the early stages, at least, the supervision of a teacher is therefore essential to point out failures in the student's self-monitoring. It is most unlikely that language laboratory exercises by themselves can remedy all of a student's faults except in a few remarkable individuals. The mere provision of a right answer, as we noted before, is not sufficient to guarantee successful learning.

3. **The training of an "inner ear"**: It is not even enough to train the student to compare his own efforts with those of a native-speaker. Our aim must finally be to enable him to compare his actual production with some inner model of what it should sound like. Self-monitoring in this more developed sense must come to represent the active side of an *Einfühlung* (infeeling) for all aspects of the language. Once again experience of the language in use, extensive listening in laboratory terms, is a vital part of the learning process.

4. **A strategy of successive approximations**: It is not reasonable to expect learners to achieve a perfect pronunciation all at once. When the length of the course permits, the teacher can guide the learner through a series of successive approximations to a standard pronunciation, concentrating at first on major impediments to intelligibility such as faulty rhythm, then establishing adequate consonant and vowel contrasts, and finally developing such features of normal speech as assimilation and the expressive use of intonation.

When the four limitations of exercises are taken into account (restricted selection, difficulties of grading, insufficiency of feedback, and failures in self-monitoring), it should be apparent that exercises by themselves are no more a complete answer to the learner's problems than drills were. Exercises must be accompanied by listening practice to give the learner experience of the language, and by problems to help him see the relevance of examples. They also require the active supervision and intervention of a teacher. But exercises can take the learner one step nearer to communication than drills do. Though they may not give him sufficient practice or sufficient information to perfect his control of structures or sound distinctions, they are always purposeful. They do not practise language points in isolation but in a context of use. There is, therefore, a better chance that something rehearsed in an exercise will be carried over into real life.

NOTES

1. "It is the constantly repeating working of the mind to make the articulated sound the expression of the thought."
   "You must therefore from finite means make an infinite use." Both remarks are from *Über die Verschiedenheit des Menschlichen Sprachbaues*, 1836.

2. G. K. Chesterton: "The Donkey".

3. For a recent recording of this, listen to the records accompanying my *Songs and Rhymes for the Teaching of English*, Longman, 1968.

4. Mr. Winston Churchill in post-war Hong Kong, and Lord Curzon in Bengal.

5. See, for instance, W. R. Lee: *Language Teaching Games and Contests*, Oxford University Press, 1965. For a still more impressive collection, see P. A. Lee-French's "Dissertation for the Diploma in English as a Second Language", Leeds University, 1964.

6. The idea of this particular laboratory game was first developed by Peter Treacher.

7. "Dissertation for the Diploma in Applied Linguistics", Edinburgh, 1966.

8. The distinction between "input" and "intake" is made by S. P. Corder in "The Significance of Learners' Errors", *International Review of Applied Linguistics*, 5, 1967.

9. F. Marty: *Language Laboratory Learning*, A–V Publications, 1960.

# 8  Problems

*At best, only a limited value*
*In the knowledge derived from experience.*
*The knowledge imposes a pattern and falsifies,*
*For the pattern is new in every moment.*
　　　　　　– T. S. ELIOT: "Four Quartets"

*The problems are solved not by giving new information,*
*but by arranging what we have always known.*
　　　　– WITTGENSTEIN: "Philosophical Investigations"

## I  The purpose of problems

Exercises and drills are aimed primarily at assimilation. They encourage
the student to use and extend what he has already learnt. They may give
him an opportunity for learning new rules, just as simply listening to or
reading passages in the language may. But they do not force him to do
this. Problems, on the other hand, are aimed primarily at accommodation,
at getting the student to formulate new rules or to modify existing ones.
Their object is to train the learner to see in the language the same patterns
and irregularities that we are aware of. His vision may at first be more
short-sighted or more richly tinged with fancy than our own.

## 2  Ashim and the plural ending

The learner's-eye view was illustrated in Chapter 2 by the misconceptions
of Shanace and Jeeto. The case of Ashim also illustrated some of the
problems that "problems" have to solve. Ashim was a seven year old pupil
who had been learning English for about six weeks. He had had about four
weeks' experience of the use of plural endings. When asked, in his mother
tongue, what this ending signified, he pointed to a car and said: *"You say*
*"car" when it's male and "cars" when it's female."*

In Ashim's mother tongue, Bengali, there are plural endings just as in
English. The only difference is that these are not used when nouns are
specifically counted: *one car, two car, three car* etc.

The plural ending only occurs when more than one object is referred to
without the precise number being stated. It is not therefore altogether
surprising that Ashim should have missed the significance of the *one car,*
*two cars* contrast in English. What is unusual is the interpretation he has
chosen for the plural ending. For grammatical gender does not exist in his
language any more than it does in English, and Bengali does not even
distinguish between masculine and feminine forms of pronouns.

In English, Ashim was early made aware that you must use *he* when
referring to a male and *she* when referring to a female. He seems to have

concluded that this distinction is observed not just in the forms of the pronoun but in the forms of all countable nouns. In the latter case, instead of adding an *s* to the beginning of the word, it is added at the end. Thus *car* must be male like *he,* and *cars* must be female like *she*.[1] We, of course, would not call them male and female if this were the case, but masculine and feminine. If Ashim had been learning Spanish, a similar set of observations about the form of pronouns, articles and some nouns would have led him to the correct identification of the gender distinction between the two words for river: *el rio* (sweet water river), *la ria* (rivermouth, estuary). Ashim's mistake is not to invent a concept of grammatical gender to account for the formal variations of a new language. It is to apply this concept to English where it is scarcely less appropriate than in his mother tongue. Had he been learning Spanish or French or Hindi, we would have applauded his perception.

Ashim's failure illustrates once again that it is the learner who invents the language, that language learning is a creative process applied to experience. What distinguishes Ashim from other learners, including the other children in his class, is not his creative imagination but his poor observation. Had he been more alert, he should have been worrying about the contrast between *boy* and *boys, girl* and *girls.* Unless the inflection implies a change of sex, it must entail a change in his ideas. Asking him to apply his rule to further examples such as these, to see if it holds good and if not why not, is a form of problem setting.

## 3  The steps in a problem

But the successful solution of the problem involves several different steps at any of which failure may occur.

**1. The learner must realise that he has made a mistake:** Ashim's mistake, like Shanace's, was one of interpretation or understanding. Any mistakes made in the Novish programme, like Jeeto's, were mistakes of analysis or production. It may not be at all easy, in practice, to make learners aware of errors of either kind. In the first place, there are often failures in self-monitoring. Secondly, the perpetration and perpetuation of the error may not interfere with successful communication. The reader would have been perfectly understood by Novish listeners, just as he can understand Jeeto. Shanace and Ashim have no difficulty in following our stories, though they may be getting some things a little skewed. But until there is a breakdown in communication, the existence of the error is not felt.

**2. The learner must see the relevance of the problem:** The problem of *boy/boys* was before Ashim's eyes all the time, but he did not see it. Even contrastive drills and games on the use of pronouns and plural forms did not succeed in drawing his attention to its relevance. Recognising what is relevant to the confirmation or falsification of a hypothesis is not just a matter of common sense, still less of applying logic. It depends partly on convention and partly on intuition. Ashim has intuitively formulated a false convention about the relevance of particular examples and the irrelevance of others. Somehow we must get him to accept our conventions and to take a second imaginative leap towards the right answer.

3. The learner must form a hypothesis: In setting a problem, the teacher anticipates what sort of false conclusions the learner might arrive at. But the learner may always form a hypothesis that the teacher had not foreseen. Problem-solving therefore requires the supervision of the teacher. His job is to determine what hypotheses the learner is actually entertaining, while the learner's job is to discover what conclusions the teacher wants him to reach. The teacher can muster further evidence to refute false hypotheses and to force the learner to think again. Making the right inference is no more a matter of logic than seeing the relevance of a problem. Beyond a certain point, we cannot help the learner. We can only tell him whether he is right or wrong. For what we are asking him to do is to see things our way, to share our knowledge of what the examples signify. Until he can intuitively match our point of view, our reasoning and definitions and explanations are likely to fall on uncomprehending ears.[2] It is not the verbal form of the rule or definition the learner has to master but its force.

4. The learner must follow the rules:[3] Nearly all the other pupils in Ashim's class were able to formulate the rule about plural endings quite correctly. But when it came to applying the rule they had invented, their behaviour was almost invariably inconsistent with it. Asked to pick up the pencils on the table, they usually picked up only one pencil. Asked to count the pencils, they would add or omit the final *s* in a whimsical way. Asked to say whether *one pencils* and *two pencil* were right or wrong when presented in contrast with the correct forms, they would often get confused. Successful discovery of a rule does not immediately lead to its implementation. A problem is only a starting point. Once it has been correctly solved, it must be followed by extensive practice. A problem develops the learner's conscious knowledge of the rules, and his understanding of the difficulties confronting him. It allows him to name them to himself, and through such identification it may help him to direct his own learning strategies and performance. But what ultimately counts is whether the rules become unconsciously assimilated.

## 4   Rules and realities

If the learner does not follow the rules that problems help him to perceive, it might be asked: *Why waste time in setting him problems at all?*

In the case of a learner such as Ashim, whose performance is seriously confused, the answer is fairly clear. There is not much point in correcting his utterances unless at the same time we help him to see *why* they are wrong. But problems can play a wider role than this. They can serve to prevent misconceptions as well as to remedy them. Suppose we follow the strategy of giving the learner extensive listening practice before we call upon him to produce a particular structure or to make a particular distinction himself. Problems can then take an intermediate place between experience and performance. They help to organise the experience in the learner's mind before he engages in a set of drills or exercises that improve his control over what he has perceived.

It could be argued that the provision of a textbook definition or rule would be less time-consuming than a problem and just as effective. With some learners this is quite possibly true. But textbook rules are not formulated in terms readily understood by younger learners, while problems can be designed to help them put their observations in their own words. Moreover, the difficulty for all learners, as I have indicated, is not to memorise the wording of a rule but to see its force. If problems can successfully encourage a learner to formulate his own rules, he can enjoy the satisfying sense of coming to grips with the language, of understanding how it works. There is, furthermore, a chance that he will remember his own rules better than the textbook's. Finally he will have learnt how to look for rules and is more likely to continue to do so in cases where the textbook offers no guidance. A recurrent theme in this book has been the need to teach the learner learning strategies, as well as structures or skills, so that he is equipped to continue to learn on his own.

The purpose of problems may now be more apparent but their limitations should not be forgotten. For the reasons discussed in the previous section, problems may fail in the object of leading the learner to the right inference. And they may still mislead the learner even when they are successful. The generalisations he makes are valuable in directing his activity. But just like the rules in a grammar book, they are almost certain to be false, at least in detail. If the learner takes the rules too literally, he will not be prepared for the occasions on which they are broken. This is not so obvious in the case of the rule about the plural ending, as every possible exception can be incorporated into the rule. The learner can only do so gradually, of course, registering and mastering each new irregularity. In the meanwhile, the very tendency to regularise will constantly tempt him into mistakes:

Ashim's hairs are black.

One nose, two nose, three nose.

I have two ears, two eyes and only one no.

But what of less clear cases, of rules that describe the use of structures as well as their formation? It is not so easy to think of learner-proof rules that distinguish the uses of different tenses in English, or the various roles of articles and modal verbs. Here we can only construct a series of *ad hoc* formulae, all too conscious that they leak. And worse still, there are some areas of usage for which it is difficult to think of any rules at all.

Even Ashim, in time, will learn to see the difference between singular and plural nouns because there is a perceptual difference in the number of discrete individuals to which they refer. Our division of time in terms of tense and aspect, of named occasions (*since, until, at, on, by* etc.) and countable intervals (*for, during, in, within* etc.) may not be so obvious to a foreign learner but we can still feel it has a conceptual basis, which can be explained to him or by him, given sufficient experience. But the rules broken below are largely irrational. If a learner makes any of the following kinds of mistake over the use of verbs of *liking:*

I like breeding a pig.

I am liking to learn English.

I like to do my homework tomorrow.

I want that he should come.

I dislike to play the tennis etc.

our reaction is usually to say: "you just don't say that", and to pass him over to drills. I think such sources of difficulty are amenable to problems, but these will be, like pronunciation problems, of a factual discovery nature. They can get him to see that things are so, but not why they are so.

# 5  Application problems

It is now time to give some examples of problems to show the principles of their design. One of the most characteristic features of a problem is that, unlike a drill, it makes use of negative as well as positive examples. The learner is given the chance of making mistakes himself or of correcting other people's. Both are tests of his control or understanding of the rules. In some problems, the likely consequences of his mistakes can be brought home to him. We can engineer situations in which faulty learning leads to a breakdown in communication, thus firmly facing the learner with the fact that he has got to think again. Such problems are mainly concerned with application or reference, and most commonly arise when there are divergences between the mother tongue and the second language.

Several sources of possible errors of this kind were illustrated in Chapter 7, section 5. A further case, particularly amenable to a problem approach, is that of colour terms in various languages. When compared to English, Bengali for instance has no distinctive names for grey and black, and a rather different distinction between green and blue. This has the effect that some objects which we would call grey are called brown, or even orange, while others which we would call blue are called green, at least by uneducated speakers. Here the learner is at his most vulnerable. He has learnt to see and name colours in terms of his own system, which seems to him both natural and necessary. In Robert Graves' phrase, *"the cool web of language winds us in".*[4] It traps us into thinking of the world as if it corresponded to our own language system. In consequence, it is difficult to see the point of other people's.

Colour terms would accordingly provide a rich area for problems for Bengali learners of English, among many others. The learner could be assigned the task of demanding objects of different colours, and be shown the consequences. A consequential approach could also be used to help Bengali learners distinguish between the English verbs *eat* and *drink*. You may remember that a single verb is employed to describe both actions. But a distinction is made between being *hungry* and being *thirsty*, and the problem (in branching form) could accordingly start from these two basic states:

*[handwritten: had or want]*

*[handwritten: mixing the two words hungry & thirsty]*

| 1. | | You're very hungry. ⟶ 2 |
|----|----|----|
| 2. | What do you say? I want to eat. ⟶ 5 I want to drink. ⟶ 3 | |
| 3. | | Here's some water. Are you happy now? No, I'm still very hungry. ⟶ 4 No, I'm still very thirsty. ⟶ 4 |
| 4. | I want to drink. ⟶ 7 I want to eat. ⟶ 5 | |
| 5. | | Here's a plate of rice. Are you happy now? No, I'm still very hungry. ⟶ 6 No, I'm still very thirsty. ⟶ 6 |
| 6. | I want to eat. ⟶ 9 I want to drink. ⟶ 7 | |
| 7. | | Here's a glass of milk. Are you happy now? No, I'm still very thirsty. ⟶ 8 No, I'm still very hungry. ⟶ 8 |
| 8. | I want to drink. ⟶ 11 I want to eat. ⟶ 9 | |

9.                                      Here's some dal (lentils). Are you happy now?

No, I'm still very thirsty.  ⟶  10

No, I'm still very hungry.  ⟶  10

---

10.     I want to eat.  ⟶  13

I want to drink.  ⟶  11

---

11.                                     Here's a bottle of coca cola. Are you happy now?

No, I'm still very hungry.  ⟶  12

No, I'm still very thirsty.  ⟶  12

---

12.     I want to drink.  ⟶  15

I want to eat.  ⟶  13

---

13.                                     Here's some fish curry. Are you happy now?

No, I'm still very thirsty.  ⟶  14

No, I'm still very hungry.  ⟶  14

---

14.     I want to drink.  ⟶  15

I want to eat.  ⟶  17

---

15.                                     Here's a cup of tea. Are you happy now?

No, I'm still very hungry.  ⟶  16

No, I'm still very thirsty.  ⟶  21

Yes, but I'm very hungry.  ⟶  2

---

16.     Try eating something.  ⟶  2

---

17.                                     Here's a chupati. Are you happy now?

No, I'm still very thirsty.  ⟶  18

No, I'm still very hungry.  ⟶  19

Yes, but I'm very thirsty.  ⟶  2

---

18.     Try drinking something.  ⟶  2

19.          You have had enough to eat. Write down the names of all the
             things you have been eating:

             .................................................

             .................................................

             .................................................

             .................................................  ⟶ 20

20.          You have been eating:

                          rice
                          dal
                          fish curry
                          and a chupati

             Now you're very thirsty.  ⟶  2

21.          You have had enough to drink. Write down the names of all the
             things you have been drinking:

                     .................................................

                     .................................................

                     .................................................

                     .................................................

                     .................................................

                     .................................................  ⟶ 22

22.          You have been drinking:

                          water
                          milk
                          coca cola
                          and tea

             You have NOT been "drinking" dal and fish curry.

             You have been ............... -ing dal and fish curry.  ⟶   23

23.          Yes, you've been *eat*ing dal and fish curry.

             You have been .......................... -ing rice and chupaties.

             You have been .......................... -ing milk and tea.

             But you haven't been.......................... -ing coffee.

             But you haven't been.......................... -ing doi (yoghurt).
             ⟶ 24

24.     You have been *eat*ing rice and chupaties.

        You have been *drink*ing milk and tea.

        You haven't been *drink*ing coffee.

        You haven't been *eat*ing doi.

        Now go to bed.

---

# 6  Intentional problems

The commentary in the last problem could also be given in the pupils' mother tongue, if necessary. At the end of the programme they could be invited to express a rule in either language. The distinction, as they will later find out, is not so much between solids and liquids, as in the manner of consumption. Semi-liquids like dal, doi and curry are eaten with a spoon (or with the fingers). We may also talk of eating thorough-going liquids like soup and sauce with a spoon. We only drink out of, or from, containers.

A similar consequential approach could be adopted for answers to the negative questions mentioned at the end of the Novish programme, viz:

1.  "Won't you have some more tea?"
    "*Yes, please*" – i.e. I'd like another cup of tea.
    "*No, thanks*" – i.e. I've had enough.

2.  "Won't you stay a little longer?"
    "*Yes, I'd love to*" – i.e. I want to stay.
    "*No, I'm sorry I can't*" – i.e. I have to go.

3.  "Isn't it raining?"
    "*Yes, it is*" – i.e. it is raining.
    "*No, it isn't*" – i.e. it is dry.

4.  "I am a fool, aren't I?"     → aren't I ?
    "*Yes, you are*" – i.e. I agree that you are a fool.
    "*No, you're not*" – i.e. I disagree that you are a fool.

5.  "You've finished this programme, haven't you?"
    "*No, not yet*" – i.e. I still have some more to do.
    "*Yes, I have*" – i.e. I am ready to do a new programme.

A new problem in identifying the speaker's intention, or the purport of what he says, might involve reactions to statements that do not mean what they say. Just as the polite and thirsty Japanese would answer *No* to the first question above, meaning to convey acceptance, so the polite but busy Bengali might phrase the second question as a request, meaning to convey rejection: *esho* (come thou).

This means: *please go*. And an equally polite guest would respond: *ashchi* (I am coming), meaning that he is going, and will probably never return. The field of polite remarks, whether sincere or insincere, is rich in material for production and comprehension problems.

## 7 Unnecessity — A problem

Without abandoning our interest in sense, we shall turn now to a structural problem. Like the eating problem, it involves selection. But this time the student must select the structure from inside his head and expose it to a critical survey:

**You are answering your friend's questions about an interview for a job. Complete the answers indicated on page 1 of your booklet:**

*1*  Q. Did you send your application by registered post?
A. *No, I didn't need to do so.*

*2*  Q. Did you enclose any photographs?
A. *No,* ........................................................

*3*  Q. Did you take all your certificates with you?
A. *No,* ........................................................

*4*  Q. Did you get there on time?
A. *Yes, but* ........................................................

*5*  Q. Did you put on a tie?
A. *No,* ........................................................

Did you notice the answer to the question about punctuality? It was:

"Yes, but I needn't have done so".

What's the difference between this and all the other answers? They were all:

"No, I didn't need to do so".

Think about it as long as you like. Write down a rule if you can. Then answer the following questions.

1. Did you send your application by registered post? Yes or no?
........ *No, you didn't.*

2. Why didn't you send it by registered post? ..............
*You didn't need to do so, it wasn't necessary.*

3. Did you put on a tie? Yes or no? ......... *No, you didn't.*

4. Why not? ................ *It wasn't necessary, you didn't need to do so.*

5. Did you get there on time? Yes or no? ......... *Yes, you did.*

6. Was it necessary for you to get there on time? Yes or no?
........... *No, it wasn't necessary, you needn't have done so, because the interviews were all postponed till next week.*

7. Need you have gone there at all? ......... *No, you needn't have done so, it wasn't necessary.*

Can you work out the rule yet? Try to do so, then complete the blanks on page 2 of your booklet. Read through it first.

1. You did go to the interview but it wasn't necessary.

.................................................................................................................

2. You didn't take all your certificates because it wasn't necessary.

.................................................................................................................

3. You didn't send any photographs because it wasn't necessary.

.................................................................................................................

4. You did take a taxi in order not to be late but it wasn't necessary.

.................................................................................................................

Fill in the blanks with either: *I didn't need to do so.* or, *I needn't have done so.*

Now show your rule to the teacher and, if he agrees with it, try to use it in the following exercises .........

The exercises could involve synonymy relations like the ones indicated immediately above, or they might involve further blank-filling where the context alone suggests whether or not an unnecessary event took place eg:

1. You.................................... all the questions, which would have saved you a lot of trouble.

2. You....................................all the questions, which saved you a lot of trouble.

The student will almost certainly need a further problem to sort out the formation rules for these two modal constructions. He will probably try to say things like:

I needn't to do so.

I needn't have to do so.

I needn't have do so etc.

A problem that would deal with these would simply require the formulation of rules that govern the distribution of categories like *infinitive, past participle* etc.

## 8  Achievement — A problem

The next problem is also a distributional one concerning the use of two modal verbs. But this time the student is given a syntactic rather than a semantic clue to the odd man out:

"**Complete the blanks on page 1 of your booklet, with the verbs** *could* **or** *managed to:*

When I was small, I was very active. I could run quickly,
I ................................jump, I .......................................skip, and I
............... climb trees. But there was one very tall tree in the park which,
for a long time, I ......................................... climb. Then one day, I
...................................... get to the top at last.

Did you get the last sentence right? *"One day I managed to get to the top at last."*

What's the difference between *could* and *managed to* in this story? See if you can work it out before you answer the following questions:

1. When you were small did you skip? Yes or no? . . . . . . .

2. Did you run about? Yes or no? . . . . . . . . *Yes, you were very active, you could skip and run about.*

3. Did you climb that tree in the park? Yes or no? . . . . . . .

4. Did you climb other trees? Yes or no? . . . . . . . . . *Yes, you could climb trees, and you even managed to climb that one one day.*

5. Did you often climb trees? Yes or no? . . . . . . .

6. Had you ever climbed that tree before? Yes or no? . . . . . . *Yes, you often climbed trees, but you had never climbed that one before.*

7. Could you climb well? . . . . . . *Yes, you could climb quite well.*

8. Then why didn't you climb that one before? . . . . . . *You couldn't climb it because it was too high,* or *too difficult.*

Do you understand the rule about *could* and *managed to* now? Write it down if you do, and then fill in the blanks on page 2. Read all the sentences first:

1. I often used to skip. I....................................... skip very well.

2. I often used to sing, but I....................................... sing very well.

3. I often climbed the tree in the park again. After the first time, I
........................... climb it quite easily.

4. I often used to run races. I .......................................run very fast.

5. On two occasions, I....................................... win the first prize for the 100 metres.

Now show your rule to your teacher and then do the following exercises . . . ."

The exercises could involve the hyponymy relationship between *could*, *managed to*, and *was able to*, the latter being used in the prompts, and one or other of the former replacing it in the responses according to whether the remainder of the prompt suggests a general ability in the past, or an achievement on specific occasions:

Replace the underlined verb in these sentences with *could* or *managed to:*

I was able to finish today's test in time.

I was able to speak English correctly before I came on this course. (etc.)

A further problem could be devised to test the learner's application of the rule in potentially ambiguous contexts. He might, for instance, be asked to say what the adverb *once* must mean in:

I once could stand on my head.

I once managed to stand on my head.

# 9 The problems of the perfect tense

Problems are like Hydra heads. No sooner is one vanquished than another seven spring forth. Nowhere is this more true than in the use of tenses in English. A number of drills in earlier chapters were concerned with the formation of one tense form, the perfect tense. They left it to the learner to discover what this tense might mean and when it should be applied. Problems could help him towards both ends. Space only permits me to sketch the objectives of a series of such problems. The problems are connected in the sense that each extends the learner's understanding of the structure. But they need not follow upon each other immediately. It would almost certainly be wiser to wait till each step is firmly consolidated before proceeding to the next one. At no point can we say that the learner has mastered the use of the tense. Rather, he is progressing towards its mastery by a series of successive approximations, just as his mastery of the sound systems of the language gradually approaches that of a native speaker.

*Step 1: Complementary distribution.* No tense form exists in isolation. It operates as part of a system. The learner should therefore study it in contrast with other tenses, chiefly the simple past, with which it is most often confused. The objective of the first problem would be to show that in certain contexts only one or the other of these could be used:

1. The messenger has just arrived.

2. The messenger arrived a few moments ago.

We cannot interchange the tense forms in these two sentences. In the first sentence we could substitute *not yet* or *already*. In the second we could substitute *yesterday, last week, a few minutes before*. The choice of tense is controlled by the time expressions. Since we cannot interchange them, we cannot say that the tenses here have any difference in meaning. They are here just distributional variants like *since* and *for*. There are, of course, other environments in which both tenses can occur, and the learner must then discover whether they have the same meaning or not.

*Step 2: Since and for.* One such environment is before a time expression beginning with the preposition *for:*

3. I lived in Edinburgh for four years.

4. I have lived in Edinburgh for four years.

Another tense form creeps in here:

5. I have been living in Edinburgh for four years.

Do these all mean different things? Sentence (3) clearly implies that I no longer live in Edinburgh, while sentences (4) and (5) imply that I still do. The last two sentences may here be synonymous. But this would not necessarily be the case with:

6. I have written letters all morning.

7. I have been writing letters all morning.

Sentence (7) may imply that I am still writing letters, while sentence (6) suggests either that I have finished altogether, or that I have stopped for the moment. The objective of problems in this second step would be to train the learner to distinguish between the use of the prepositions *since* and *for,* and to discover the implications of the different tense-forms that may occur with the latter.

*Step 3: Implicit time reference.* In the previous examples there has been an explicit reference to time in the form of an adverb or time expression. What happens when these are omitted?

8. Napoleon has won the battle of Borodino.

9. Napoleon won the battle of Borodino.

Both sentences imply that the battle is over. But the first creates a sense of immediacy, whether this is because the battle has just ended, or because the speaker wants to carry his audience back in time to a point when this would have been so. In the latter case the contrast between the two tenses becomes stylistic rather than referential. The objective of problems at this stage would be to make the learner aware of the effects of different tenses employed in narrative.

*Step 4: On-going states.* In contrast with the previous two examples, the perfect tense might indicate that something has not yet ended:

10. Natasha married Pierre.

11. Natasha has married Pierre.

The ceremony is over in both cases, but the state of wedlock is still operative in the second. To the first sentence we might add that she divorced him later. By the second tense they are united for ever. We cannot follow it up with: .... *but she has divorced him since then.*

The objective of problems at this stage must be to make the learner see that the acts of vowing, agreeing, adopting, swearing (to do something), upsetting, humiliating, frightening, surprising etc., remain continuously operative or effective in the perfect tense. But oddly enough *living* doesn't.

12. I have lived in Edinburgh too,

now suggests that I am no longer living there.

*Step 5: Effective acts.* The perfect tense may indicate, on the other hand, that something has not yet been done.

13. Lady Macbeth persuaded me to murder Duncan.

14. Lady Macbeth has persuaded me to murder him.

The first sentence surely indicates that I have done so, the second that I have yet to do so. The objective of problems at this stage is to indicate to the learner that other kinds of acts, such as convincing or tempting people to do things, also remain unfulfilled in the perfect tense.[5]

*Step 6: Free variation.* There are contexts in which the two tense forms, and others, may be in free variation. Suppose, on hearing Macbeth confess, I were to say:

15. He told us the truth.

16. He has told us the truth.

17. He has been telling us the truth.

18. He is telling us the truth.

In these circumstances, the choice of tense makes little or no difference to the import of my remarks. All of them refer to a confession that has already been made, and indicate my opinion of its validity. If the confession were true at the time, it is true now and for ever. Problems at this stage must show the learner how far he too can choose his tense forms freely.

*Step 7: Complementary distribution again.* There are still other contexts in which only one tense form can occur.

19. Are you still going to the Capitol?
    *No, I've been.*

20. Is Desdemona still your wife?
    *No, she was.*

21. It's time you got your tenses sorted out.

*"No, I went"* would be just as impossible an answer to the first question as *"No, she has been"* would be to the second. The perfect tense

could not be used in the third example either, in which the past tense perversely refers to a *future* action. The objective of problems at this stage would be to fill in gaps in the learner's knowledge, to show him how to answer questions elliptically and how to interpret or employ idiomatic expressions.

The examples given in these seven steps are merely indicative of the kind of material that could be exploited in problems. My intention was to show that a tense-form, such as the perfect tense, is not something that can be mastered in a couple of lessons. The learner must rather progress by a series of successive approximations, at one step learning the form of the tense and its relationship with prepositions and adverbs of time, at another coming to understand its differing implications when applied to different classes of verb, and finally accustoming himself to small anomalies in its usage. At each stage he will need extensive practice in the form of comprehension and production exercises. But the introduction to each step might well take the form of a problem. For each step requires the learner to re-organise or extend his ideas of what the tense may mean.

How far problems help the learner to accommodate new concepts can be put to the test in the next sample. This is another lesson in Bengali in the form of a linear programme. Its purpose is to introduce the reader, in a rudimentary way, to the contrasting forms and uses of the past and perfect tenses.

## 10   Negation in Bengali — A problem

*Imagine that you are living in Calcutta and beginning to learn Bengali. You have a Bengali friend who is helping you. He allows you to ask questions in English but always answers in his mother tongue to develop your understanding. After a little you notice that something odd happens when he answers questions in the negative. To determine what is going on, you put a series of questions. At each step, stop to think about the form his answers take, before asking some more questions.*

1.  "Would you like me to speak in Bengali?"----"hā."

    "Will you answer me in English?" ----"na."

    *What do you think the answers* hā *and* na *mean?*

---

2.  *Yes and no. But you persist:*

    "If I give you the money, will you buy me some mangoes?"---"hā, kinbo."

    "If I give you the money, will you buy me an English newspaper?"---"na, kinbo na".

    *What is the tense of the verbs in his answers, and how would you translate the second occurrence of* na *in the second?*

---

3. *The tense is future, and* na *can be translated by* not *as well as* no. *The verb* kena *of course means* to buy.

"Do you buy mangoes very often?"---"hā, kini."

"Have you got any English newspapers?"---"na, kini na."

"Have you got any whisky?"---"na, kini ni."

> *What is the tense of the verbs in these answers, and how would you translate* ni *in the last one?*

---

4. kini *is the first person singular of the present tense of* kena. *Your friend means that he often buys mangoes but he doesn't buy English newspapers.* ni *would also be translated as* not *in the last sentence. Are* ni *and* na *then free variants like* not *and* n't *in English? Let's see:*

"Are there any mangoes in the house now?"---"hā, kinechi."

"Is there any doi?"---"na, kini ni."

> *What is the tense of the verbs in these two answers?*

---

5. kinechi *is the first person singular of the perfect tense. Your friend has bought some mangoes. How would he indicate that he hadn't bought any? Complete this answer with the perfect tense of the verb:*

> na,

---

6. na, kini ni. *Yes,* kini ni *is the negative form of the perfect tense. It is most confusing that the verb appears to be in the present tense. So* ni *and* na *are not free variants. They indicate a change in tense.* kinechi na *would be ungrammatical. What next?*
"Have you bought any lichees today?"---"ha, kinlam."

"Have you got today's *Statesman?*"---"na, kinlam na."

"Have you got any back numbers of *The Times?*"---"na, kini ni."

> *What is the tense of these three verbs?*

---

7. kinlam *is the first person of the past tense of the verb. You may remember that this tense is preferred when an action took place in the immediate past. Use this information to translate the following sentences into Bengali. The verb* to read *or* study *has the stem* por *which can be used with appropriate endings in all the examples:*

1. (often) read. ami

2. I do not study. ami

3. I will read (it). ami

4. I will not study (it). ami

5. I have read (it already). ami

6. I have not (yet) read (it). ami

7. I have (just) read (it). ami

8. I did not read (it recently). ami

9. I did not read (it at that time). ami

---

8. 1. ami poṛi.

   2. ami poṛi na.

   3. ami poṛbo.

   4. ami poṛbo na.

   5. ami poṛechi.

   6. ami poṛi ni.

   7. ami poṛlam.

   8. ami poṛlam na.

   9. ami poṛi ni.

*Can you formulate a rule governing the use of past and perfect tenses in Bengali, and the use of* ni *and* na? *The time expressions in the brackets of frame 7 are vital clues to the choice of tense.*

---

9. *You may have realised that* ni *following an apparently present tense form optionally negates the past as well as the perfect tense.* poṛi ni *is thus ambiguous as regards tense, and never a free variant of* poṛi na. *One last question: how would your friend answer in the negative:*

"Do you read the English newspapers?"----"na, ami.............................."

10. *Your friend might say:*

     na, ami poṛi ne.

*Is* ne *a free variant of* ni *or* na?

11. ne *is a free variant in some dialects of* na, *but not of* ni, *when the present tense refers to a habitual action.*

---

## 11   The design of problems

The Bengali problem of the last section involved one of the most difficult tasks in language teaching: to establish a fairly subtle distinction for a reader who is assumed to have no previous experience of the language.

Even if the example did not totally succeed, several points about the design of problems may have become more apparent.

**(1) The learner starts from the familiar.** To a genuine learner of Bengali most of the tense forms would already have been familiar. It is their conflation in the negative which he may find puzzling. Similarly in the problem about *could* and *managed to* it is assumed that the learner has already had experience of at least one, or perhaps both, verbs. The mistake he is likely to make is to use them interchangeably in contexts where only one would be appropriate.

**(2) The problem proceeds by a series of traps.** The learner is set a number of small tests. If he fails in a test, he cannot help realising that he has something to learn. The tests must cover every aspect of form or usage over which the learner is likely to err. By making a mistake in the course of a problem, he not only has the opportunity of putting it right himself, but of discovering why it was wrong. Problems are an application of a principle earlier discussed: to find out the difference between right and wrong, we must occasionally do something wrong.

**(3) The learner is invited to describe his observations and to formulate a rule in his own terms.** It is important to encourage the learner to put things in his own words for several reasons previously discussed. He may not be accustomed to the grammatical terminology we employ. He may think he understands a given rule when a formulation of his own would reveal that there were still aspects misunderstood. Finally he may remember his own rules better than ours and continue to look for rules on his own. The understanding of principles and the formulation of rules are the immediate object of problems. They are, it has already been noted, only an intermediate aid in language learning. Ultimate success depends not on the rules being followed to the letter, but on their becoming unnecessary: the learner can perform correctly without bothering to think why or how.

NOTES

1. Ashim could read all these words and, like most Indian children, he spells them out alphabetically rather than phonically, i.e. *"S, H, E – she"*.
2. "If language is to be a means of communication, there must be an agreement not only in definitions but in judgements" – L. Wittgenstein, *Philosophical Investigations*, Blackwell, 1958.
3. For a full discussion of what the expressions "knowing a rule", "following a rule", might and might not mean, see Wittgenstein, *Philosophical Investigations*, op. cit.
4. There is a great deal of literature on this subject in prose as well as verse. See for instance, E. T. Hall: *The Silent Language*, Fawcett Publications Connecticut, 1961; E. H. Lenneberg and J. M. Roberts: "The Language of Experience", in *Psycholinguistics*. ed. Saporta, Holt, Rinehart and Winston, 1961, J. B. Carroll: "Lin-

guistic Relativity, Contrastive Linguistics and Language Learning", *International Review of Applied Linguistics* Vol. 1, No. 1, 1963; and J. Nicholls: "A Survey of Writing and Experiment in the Field of Ethnolinguistics", Dissertation for the Diploma in General Linguistics, Edinburgh, 1965.

5. A fuller list of "performative verbs", and their varying implications in different grammatical contexts, is given in J. L. Austin: *How to do Things with Words,* Oxford University Press, 1962.

# 9 A strategy for the language laboratory

*We shall not cease from exploration*
*And the end of all our exploring*
*Will be to arrive where we started*
*And know the place for the first time.*
     – T. S. ELIOT: "Four Quartets"

## 1 Principles and personalities

This book set out to investigate two questions:

1. What can be done in the language laboratory?

2. Is laboratory practice more effective than classroom work?

Various chapters have now dealt with what can be done in the laboratory. I have tried to define the purpose, the possibilities and the limitations of several distinct forms of practice. The second question has not yet been answered. The effectiveness of laboratory work is still something that requires experimental investigation. Every teacher, moreover, is entitled to undertake his own experiments and to trust in his own findings. Even if existing research were more conclusive, it necessarily ignores an imponderable factor – the tastes and aptitudes of each particular teacher and each particular learner. Some teachers may find, for example, that the laboratory accords ill with their teaching style and personality, while others respond enthusiastically to the chance of exploring its resources. Some learners may delight in working on their own with aural material, while others may never overcome their bewilderment with the machinery.

Because teaching and learning both depend as much on personality as on principle, the second question can never receive more than partial or relative answers. With these cautions, just one such relative answer will be attempted in this chapter. It is not founded on controlled research. Its only authority is a certain amount of trial and error, an early and continuing harvest of errors having led to frequent modifications in this personal rationale of the language laboratory.

## 2 The effectiveness of the laboratory

The question about the effectiveness of the language laboratory can be taken in two parts:

1. Do learners who do not need to speak need to use the laboratory?

2. Do learners who do need to speak need to use it?

Many of the principles, and all the drills and exercises illustrated, were concerned with the problems of getting the learner to listen or to speak. The language laboratory has been considered as a means of providing or eliciting the spoken word. But, in many parts of the world where English (for example) is learnt as a second language, the learner's primary contact with it is through the written word. Some experts would argue that this does not make the laboratory superfluous: to read and write, they maintain, you must first be able to speak, and the laboratory is an effective means of practising speech.

The first part of this argument is open to question. Michael West, in his long term survey of this issue, found that it was better to divorce the acquisition of reading and that of spoken skills from a very early stage. Reading could then develop freely at its own, much quicker pace.[1] To understand what we read, we do not need to understand every word or to have active control over all the vocabulary and structural devices whose sense we can guess from the context.

This does not mean that the language laboratory has no part to play in learning to read. For the learner interested in, or already familiar with, the spoken language, the use of "taped" reading materials may be of the greatest value. Blind English children have been helped to read with the Language Master, a tape-reading machine that allows them to follow the shapes of the letters with their fingers at the same time as hearing the sounds through their ears. Many more fortunate learners might benefit from being able to associate what they see with what they hear. The tape-recorder can give reading an aural dimension which may be particularly useful in the early stages. Eventually the learner must come to read silently and by himself.

Knowing how to speak may not be essential for learning how to read and write. But knowing how to read and write is a valuable aid for learning to speak. Children, of course, learn to talk their mother tongue before they learn to read. They have more time at their disposal than we can usually afford and their aural memory may be more receptive than ours. The principal problem which the language laboratory is supposed to meet is the problem of remembering. By repeated practice the learner is helped not to forget what has been orally introduced in the classroom. But unless he has a particularly good aural memory, it is likely that the aural-oral interchanges of the laboratory will be more forgettable than any form of written practice. The characteristic of the spoken word is its ephemerality. Writing preserves rules, examples and responses in a form that can be consulted or revised whenever the need arises. The written word can either reinforce the spoken word, as in many of my examples, or it could replace it altogether.

It might be argued that, although written practice helps the learner to remember, it does not give him a chance to talk. But nor, for different reasons, does the laboratory. If we take speech to mean spontaneous conversation, the end of all our endeavours, this is the one thing that cannot be done with a tape-recorder. It can only be simulated. And if we feel it is worth simulating speech in the air, we must also consider whether it might not be equally or more effectively simulated on paper.

*Speaking a language,* in Wittgenstein's words, *is part of an activity, or a form of life.* Doing a drill or an exercise in the laboratory is certainly an activity, but it can be difficult to bring to life. Doing a branching programme, undertaking project work in the classroom, or simply watching television where this is possible, may each in different ways make the language more alive in the pupil's mind.

Two points have been argued so far:

(i) there are some language activities, such as reading and writing, in which the language laboratory at the most has only a marginal, though possibly beneficial, part to play.

(ii) there are no language activities which can safely be left entirely to the language laboratory, unless the pupil also has the benefit of written texts or exercises, and the possibility of conversing with a teacher or with other fluent speakers.

The question from which I started has still to be answered. Which activities, if any, can be more effectively practised in the laboratory than in the classroom? The different forms of practice can now be considered in turn:

**1. Listening practice**: It is doubtful whether most learners get enough listening practice in the classroom. The teacher can, of course, read to them, tell them stories, give instructions or explanations, and discuss topics of interest. But unless he is a native speaker, the laboratory can offer the only prolonged opportunity of listening to native voices. Such a facility is of major importance when the learner's object is to understand or imitate native speakers. The learner can, moreover, stop the tape whenever he wishes and replay difficult sections as often as necessary. If a library of tapes is also available, each learner can choose what he wants to listen to as well as proceed at his own pace. The only limitations on what can be learnt from listening in the laboratory are the acoustic quality of the tapes and the lack of a corresponding visual image — which only television, film or real life can supply. If these two deficiencies can be counter-balanced as far as possible in the design of listening tapes, the laboratory is likely to prove richer and more effective for some kinds of listening practice than the classroom. Sadly this use of the laboratory has been rather neglected and little material is commercially available.

**2. Comprehension exercises**: To develop his understanding of the spoken language through aural assignments, the learner may once more wish to listen to the same passage several times, or in chunks of varying sizes. It is tedious for the teacher in the classroom to repeat himself again and again like a tape-recorder, and he cannot, if he does so, allow for differences in individual pupils' needs, interests, and pace of work. Though the same limitations apply to comprehension exercises in the laboratory as to simple listening materials, the laboratory may once again justify its use. Several courses are moreover available on the market which the teacher might be able to adopt or adapt for his own purposes.

**3. Production exercises:** The laboratory offers the learner the chance of unlimited repetition and role-playing exercises, though the effectiveness of both will be dependent on his ability to monitor himself. He can work on his own at his own materials, and the laboratory gives him far more time in which to practise than he will be able to get in the classroom where he has to wait for other pupils to have their turn. For pronunciation practice and training in oral fluency the laboratory is accordingly likely to prove more effective than the classroom. This is not so clearly the case with the more ambitious kinds of exercises outlined in Chapter 7. When specific language skills are being developed, a written exercise may allow just as much intensive individual practice in a more convenient, less time-consuming, and more memorable form. The disadvantage of the laboratory is that the linear nature of the tape does not allow differential treatment for different learners — unless the number of different tapes is multiplied in proportion to the number of pupils. Existing tape-recorders are clumsy and expensive means of presenting branching programmes, which are easy to reproduce in type or print. I have tried to show, in my examples, that it is the branching programme that, above all other forms of practice, caters to individual differences and helps the learner to learn from his mistakes. Such a programme simulates the give and take of real communication more closely than a simple tape can ever do. At present neither branching programmes nor taped exercises are widely available on the market.

**4. Problems:** The laboratory possesses the same advantages and disadvantages with respect to problems except that the need for leisure, reflection, a visual presentation, and a branching progression may be still more pressing. Only in the case of pronunciation problems is an aural presentation equally urgent. Problems have always been devised by teachers in an *ad hoc* way. But so far nobody has published taped materials that are based on a problem approach.

**5. Drills:** A wide variety of drills, on the other hand, have been produced commercially. Some of these are for pronunciation practice, some for structural work. In practice, as we have seen, structural drills may train the learner to do little more than string syllables together. The language laboratory once again gives him the chance to do so intensively on his own, but more might be learnt about the use of structures through intelligent drilling in the classroom. And the content of the drills might be better remembered if the students produced their responses in writing. Some learners, however, enjoy mechanical practice in the laboratory, even if the teacher rapidly gets bored with it. They feel it gives them confidence and a sense of familiarity in the oral language.

## 3 Two strategies of laboratory use

These comments on the effectiveness of the laboratory in different areas may strike the reader as perverse. For it is in the fields that have been least exploited commercially that I have suggested laboratory work is most promising. In those that have been most thoroughly tested, the results have often been disappointing or disproportionate to the time and cost involved. To the reader who wants to experiment in designing his own materials, I can suggest a choice of strategies. The "fail-safe" course is to adapt Polonius' advice: *Give every tape thine ear but few thy voice.*

A teacher who invests his time and tapes in designing listening materials and comprehension exercises is most likely to reap the benefits of the special facilities afforded by the laboratory. If simple repetition exercises are added, he still has a strategy of laboratory use that can be followed with learners of all kinds and all ages. In this strategy, the laboratory is a combination of listening library and individual repetition trainer. It gives the learner the chance of listening to the language being spoken, of developing his aural understanding, and of gaining oral confidence through repetition practice. In these three areas individual practice is essential. In the laboratory it can be more intensive than in the classroom, as well as more fully under the individual student's own control. Properly designed and adequately supervised work in the laboratory has accordingly every chance of being more effective than similar classroom practice. Time in the classroom can then be devoted to preparing for laboratory sessions, to exploiting them, and to developing skills such as conversation which cannot be so confidently entrusted to the laboratory. Notice that for the purposes of this strategy a full-scale language laboratory such as that outlined in Chapter 1, section 2, is not necessary. For listening practice and aural comprehension the student does not need to record his own voice. Even for repetition practice this facility may not be essential as long as the student can repeat the exercise till he is satisfied with his performance. The minimum that is required is a separate playdeck for each student so that he can select his own tape and stop it or replay it when he wants. If the teacher is further willing to forego the advantages of fully individualised practice, a single tape-recorder (with or without multiple headsets) is sufficient to control choral repetition and group listening practice. This still exacts individual effort from the learner but, as in normal classroom work, does not permit particular pupils to work at their own pace on their own problems.

The "fail-safe" strategy is economic in its use of the laboratory and relatively economical in the nature of the equipment it requires. The alternative is to explore every possible use of a fully equipped laboratory to discover what can profitably be practised there. Since exercises and problems are scarce on the market, the teacher will have to make up his own. The chapters on these themes in this book were intended to indicate some of the lines he could investigate. While it cannot be claimed that all these sample materials would be more effectively employed in the laboratory than in the classroom, they might well be just as effective there.

It is time to stress that laboratory and classroom are not so much mutually exclusive as complementary. A teacher who has a laboratory and time to devote to it is rather like a teacher who has a good library. He has an extra facility, but it is up to him to find the best uses for it. Laboratory work, just like library assignments, requires preparation in class and adequate follow-up. And like a library, a laboratory creates variety in instruction.

Variety might almost be promoted to a principle of learning. All too often textbooks seem to take it for granted that learners learn in the same way and require no more than a handful of practice techniques. Experience suggests the contrary. Different learners respond to different approaches from an early age, but all of them benefit from variety. Some learners may be especially stimulated by laboratory work and give more of their attention to it than they would to identical exercises in the classroom. Even drills can become interesting or profitable when they are used in due proportion. What reduces the effectiveness of any approach is lack of choice. An exclusive diet of drills, just like an exclusive reliance on the laboratory, is likely to lead to boredom among most pupils and unnecessary frustration in some.

The language laboratory, then, promotes variety in three distinct ways. It can make a change from the classroom even when similar materials are being used in both. If it is not to become a chore, the laboratory itself should be used in a variety of ways and with as rich as possible a variety of materials. Finally, it permits variation in task and pace of work among the pupils. In the next section we shall consider how desirable individual practice is and how far it is usually achieved in practice.

## 4 The value of individual practice

We have been considering the laboratory as an aid in learning to talk. The first part of this process, learning, is individual. The second part, talking, is not. Much is rightly made of how the laboratory facilitates individual practice. In contrast to oral practice in the classroom, the learner can be actively responding all the time. He can control the pace of his own learning, and he can control the materials he studies. This is the theory at least. In practice, a four-phase drill, in a laboratory with recording facilities, allows the learner to take an active part for something less than a quarter of the time. The rest of the session he spends waiting for the next prompt, listening to the last response, playing back his own voice, or trying to find the place on the tape. In some laboratories, he is not allowed to control the pace of the tape, and in nearly all he has to use the same materials as the rest of his class, irrespective of his abilities, needs or interests. Commercially prepared courses may restrict rather than significantly increase the opportunities for individual treatment. This is because it is not commercially viable to produce different materials for different students. A tape already costs more than a book and teaching institutions have only limited funds for purchasing either.

The individual teacher with sufficient time and a supply of blank tape is not in quite the same position as a publisher. He can afford to prepare materials that are not going to be used by all his class. He can also prepare alternative versions of the same materials for different pupils. He can further arrange his lessons so that individual pupils as far as possible can work at their own rate. This is doubtless extravagant in terms of teaching time and effort. The question is whether it is worthwhile in terms of what is learnt. Since only lip-service has hitherto been paid to individual assignments in the laboratory, it is impossible to predict what the gains might be. But it should be remembered that the very facilities for which the laboratory has been most vaunted are those that, for reasons of time and expense, have been least explored.

Although much has yet to be discovered about the value of individual practice, it should also be remembered that learning in isolation is not necessarily more effective for all purposes. Learning takes place in the individual but it can be encouraged by the group. Problems, drills, exercises and even listening practice can all at times benefit from the co-operation of a group.[2] Pairs of learners or small teams can pool their resources, correct each other's suggestions, and, most desirable of all, explain things to each other. Genuine conversation is impossible in the laboratory. It can only be practised with the teacher or among the students. An intelligent use of teamwork can bring conversation to the door of the laboratory and, if the pupils are able to work together on taped materials, can even bring it inside.

## 5 Envoi

The effective use of the laboratory thus depends on a balance of expedients, a combination of ingenuity and a capacity for taking pains. The laboratory is not likely to mean less work for the teacher but more. And he can seldom escape from the uncertainty that things might not be better done in another way or through another means. Just because the laboratory is costly and time-consuming, we are forced to ask what it can do that we cannot do so well. To the extent that we can answer this question one way or the other, we are discovering something about the conditions that promote learning. To the extent that we cannot, we must admit that we are still in the dark about the nature of language learning and of the learner. Wittgenstein characterises the learner's task in these words: *To imagine a language means to imagine a form of life.*

Somehow, on the basis of what we present to him, the learner has to imagine our language, its rules and irregularities, the form of life which it reflects and engenders. And if we are to understand his mistakes and difficulties, or to make the best uses of the resources at our command, we have to imagine him, a strange form of life in himself, with his own evolving form of language, reflecting his own manner of becoming.

*When the tide ebbs we can see the layout of the land. When emotion clear out we can see the rights & wrongs g human behaviour.*

**NOTES**

1. See M. West: *Learning to Read a Foreign Language,* Longman, first published 1926, new edition 1941.
2. See, for example, K. Austwick: "Report of an experiment comparing paired and individual programming", *New Education,* August 1965.

*Ear Drops*
*Neurobeon*
*Tia R Bank A/c*
*Money for Armando*
*Records.*

*Slade*       *Mrs Julie Costa*
*DDT*          *Mr Quadros.*
*Tailor An eraser*
*Combs a cushion,*
*        Mrs Berta Menezs*
*Phenergam Bolt.*
*        glasses*
*        Nails*
*        watch*
*        & Enthusiasm*
*        Glam.*
*        Air letter*

*Dropping out bad friends cuts out a lot of waste g time.*